THE ECONOMICS OF CONSTITUTIONAL LAW AND PUBLIC CHOICE

By

David W. Barnes
Professor of Law, University of Denver

Lynn A. Stout
Professor of Law, Georgetown University

Reprinted from Barnes and Stout's "Cases and Materials on LAW AND ECONOMICS" (West, 1992)

AMERICAN CASEBOOK SERIES ®

WEST PUBLISHING CO.
ST. PAUL, MINN., 1992

Reprinted from Barnes and Stout's "Cases and Materials on LAW AND ECONOMICS" (West, 1992).

American Casebook Series, and the WP symbol are registered trademarks of West Publishing Co. Registered in the U.S. Patent and Trademark Office.

Library of Congress Cataloging-in-Publication Data

Barnes, David W.
The economics of constitutional law and public choice / by David W. Barnes, Lynn A. Stout.
p. cm. — (American casebook series)
Includes index.
ISBN 0–314–01118–8
1. United States—Constitutional law—Cases. 2. United States—Constitutional law—Economic aspects. 3. United States—Constitutional law—Social aspects. 4. Social choice—United States. I. Stout, Lynn A., 1957– . II. Title. III. Series.
KF4549B25 1991
342.73—dc20
[347.302] 92–20867
CIP

ISBN 0–314–01118–8

(B. & S.) Const'l ACB

Preface

During the past three decades, scholars wielding the tools of economics have marched through the curricula of American law schools, applying economic analysis to one substantive area of law after another. Accustomed to formal theoretical models of institutions and human behavior, "law and economics" scholars often examine legal rules in the abstract rather than discussing their application to specific cases. By contrast, conventional law teaching begins with specific cases and abstracts from those cases the general principles governing decisions. The series of books of which this one is a part combines the theory of economics and the pedagogy of law by exploring economic analysis of law primarily through reported judicial opinions and agency decisions. Excerpts from classic writings have been included to give a flavor for the type of discourse in which law and economics scholars engage.

Economic analysis is becoming a routine part of the consideration of policies underlying various substantive areas of law. This series provides cases and materials to supplement law school courses in which economic analysis is particularly relevant. Three books, *The Economics of Property Rights and Nuisance Law, The Economic Analysis of Tort Law*, and *The Economics of Contract Law*, focus on the economic analysis of common law courses typically taught in the first year of law school. *Economic Foundations of Regulation and Antitrust Law* presents an introduction to microeconomic theory in the context of government regulation of business, including cases and materials raising issues of occupational safety and health, environmental regulation, postal regulation, cable television, and consumer protection, along with tax and antitrust cases. *The Economics of Constitutional Law and Public Choice* examines constitutional questions of equal protection, due process, separation of powers, voting rights, the police power, and judicial review, among others. All of the books in the series are designed for readers with no prior economic training.

The Economics of Constitutional Law and Public Choice is a particularly exciting addition to the law and economics literature. It introduces the emerging field of "public choice" and applies public choice theory to cases involving a wide array of constitutional issues. The book examines the economic justifications for a coercive state, the economic and distributional implications of using legislative voting to make collective decisions, and the economic logic of constitutional devices such as separation of powers, an independent judiciary, and special protections for the political and property rights of individuals and oppressed classes.

The case orientation of these books should appeal to those eager to escape the artificial assumptions often associated with economics, as well as those eager to explore the ethical and distributional dimensions of law. Analyzing reported decisions requires economics to come to grips with reality. In some circumstances, the assumptions made to facilitate economic analysis seem clearly implausible. Factual contexts also highlight the distributional and ethical implications of economic analysis of law. Rather than gloss over such issues, the books in the series regularly raise the normative implications of particular legal rules. *The Economics of Property Rights and Nuisance Law,* for instance, considers the efficiency and distributional implications of alternative forms of property rights and of different methods of protecting property rights. *The Economic Analysis of Tort Law* draws the reader's attention to the distributional implications of alternative measures of damages. *The Economics of Contract Law* considers contract law's bias in favor of the status quo from which bargaining takes place and the implications of unequal bargaining power. *Economic Foundations of Regulation and Antitrust Law* contrasts an antitrust policy that focuses on allocative efficiency to a policy that focuses on the welfare of consumers as a class. The analysis of constitutional law in *The Economics of Constitutional Law and Public Choice* highlights the distribution of power among society's members and the distributional implications of alternative mechanisms for institutionalizing state coercion. These books are vehicles for appreciating and critically examining, rather than merely promoting, the economic analysis of law.

Most footnotes and citations contained in reported opinions and other quoted materials have been omitted without any indication. In the rare occasions where such footnotes have been included, they are reproduced with their original numbering. All other omissions from excerpted texts are indicated by asterisks.

Acknowledgments

The authors would like to thank the publishers and authors of the following works for allowing them to include excerpts in this text or in *Cases and Materials on LAW AND ECONOMICS*, from which this text is derived:

J. Buchanan & G. Tullock, The Calculus of Consent: Logical Foundations of Constitutional Democracy 63–72, 77–78, 81 (1962). Copyright © 1962 by the University of Michigan Press. Reprinted with permission.

Calabresi and Melamed, Property Rules, Liability Rules, and Inalienability: One View of the Cathedral. 85 Harv.L.Rev. 1089, 1092–93, 1105, 1111–15 (1972). Copyright © 1972 by the Harvard Law Review Association. Reprinted with permission.

Coase, The Problem of Social Cost, 3 J. Law & Econ. 1–2, 13 (1960). Copyright © 1960 by the University of Chicago, University of Chicago Press. Reprinted with permission.

Easterbrook, Ways of Criticizing the Court, 95 Harv.L.Rev. 802, 811–16, 818–19, 831 (1982). Copyright © 1982 by the Harvard Law Review Association. Reprinted with permission.

Hardin, The Tragedy of the Commons, 162 Science 1243, 1244–45 (December 13, 1968). Copyright © 1968 by the American Association for the Advancement of Science. Reprinted with permission.

Posner, Gratuitous Promises in Economics and Law, 6 J. Legal Studies 411–13 (1977). Copyright © 1977 by the University of Chicago, University of Chicago Press. Reprinted with permission.

Priest, The Common Law Process and the Selection of Efficient Rules, 6 J. Legal Studies 65–73, 81–82 (1977). Copyright © 1977 by the University of Chicago, University of Chicago Press. Reprinted with permission.

J. Rawls, A Theory of Justice 3–4, 11, 12, 13, 14–15, 22, 60–62, 136–37, 140–41, 151–53 (1971). Copyright © 1971 by the President and Fellows of Harvard College, Harvard University Press. Reprinted with permission.

Shavell, Strict Liability Versus Negligence, 9 J. Legal Studies 1–3, 22–23 (1980). Copyright © 1980 by the University of Chicago, University of Chicago Press. Reprinted with permission.

Williamson, Economics As An Antitrust Defense Revisited, 125 U.Pa.L.Rev. 699, 704, 706–708 (1977). Copyright © 1977 by The University of Pennsylvania. Reprinted with permission.

*

Summary of Contents

*

Table of Contents

THE ECONOMICS OF CONSTITUTIONAL LAW AND PUBLIC CHOICE

*

Table of Cases

The principal cases are in bold type. Cases cited or discussed in the text are roman type. References are to pages. Cases cited in principal cases and within other quoted materials are not included.

*

THE ECONOMICS OF CONSTITUTIONAL LAW AND PUBLIC CHOICE

*

INTRODUCTION

Most law students have had some exposure, either as undergraduates or in law school, to the basic precepts of economic analysis. This introduction provides a brief overview of the most important economic concepts for those who have not.

Economics is the study of rational choice in a world of scarcity. Economists assume that rational people desire happiness, satisfaction, or well-being (what economists term *utility*). Rational individuals can increase their happiness by using their limited resources *efficiently*—that is, by allocating scarce resources so as to extract the maximum possible utility from them. Other things being equal, an efficient world where resources are allocated to maximize the happiness extracted from them is preferable to an inefficient world where less happiness is extracted from the same resources. If Jane gets 5 units of happiness (utils) from going to the opera but 10 utils from attending a baseball game, while John gets 10 utils from opera but only 5 utils from baseball, a world where baseball tickets are allocated to Jane and opera tickets are allocated to John is preferable to a world where the reverse is true.

Unfortunately, it is difficult to measure aggregate levels of happiness without comparing one person's level of utility to another's. (Note how the above example assumes that 5 utils reflects the same amount of happiness for John or Jane). Because no direct means of measuring Jane's and John's actual utility levels exists, some economists who wish to avoid interpersonal comparisons of utility levels employ the *Pareto criteria* for determining whether a reallocation of resources is efficient. A reallocation is *Pareto superior* if it leaves at least one person better off while leaving no one worse off. Thus, if baseball buff Jane has opera tickets and opera-loving John has baseball tickets, a voluntary exchange between the two is Pareto superior because at least one party (and in this case both) is made better off while no one is made worse off. If, however, the baseball tickets are taken forcibly from John and given to Jane, that reallocation would fail the Pareto criteria for efficiency and be *Pareto inferior* because it leaves at least one person (John) worse off.

The Pareto criteria are quite strict: many resource reallocations leave at least one person worse off than before. Economists who desire a less strict test of efficiency often adopt the *Kaldor-Hicks* test of efficiency, which holds that a reallocation is efficient if the winners who gain the resource would be willing to pay an amount of money sufficient to fully compensate the losers (the compensation need not be actually paid). The Kaldor-Hicks criteria essentially measures the utility different individuals extract from different resources according to their willingness to pay for those resources. If Jane is willing to pay $10 for baseball tickets while John is only willing to pay $5, it is efficient to forcibly take the tickets from John and give them to Jane because she would be willing to pay an amount (up to $10) for the tickets which would fully compensate John for his loss ($5). Economists also describe such reallocations as *wealth-maximizing,* because they increase social "wealth"—that is, the value of society's resources as measured by people's willingness to pay money for them.

The Kaldor-Hicks or wealth-maximization test of efficiency makes interpersonal comparisons of utility by assuming that one dollar provides the same amount of utility to Jane as it does to John. Thus, if Jane is willing to sacrifice $10 for the tickets while John is only willing to pay $5, we assume Jane must expect to extract more utility from the tickets. There are some circumstances, however, where it seems unreasonable to assume that different people extract the same amount of utility from a dollar. For most people, money seems to provide *declining marginal utility*: the more dollars you have, the less value you attach to each additional dollar. Thus a very poor person is likely to gain greater happiness from a gift of $1 than a millionaire would.

The notion of declining marginal utility for money underlies the concept of *risk aversion.* To the economist, risk simply means variation or uncertainty: a 50% chance of receiving $1 million is more risky than a certainty of receiving $500,000. Declining marginal utility for money leads to risk aversion because people value the dollars they lose more than they value the dollars they gain. A risk-averse individual will choose a certainty of receiving $500,000 over a 50% chance of receiving a million because she values her first $500,000 more than her second, and is unwilling to accept a 50% chance of losing the first $500,000 for a 50% chance of gaining the second $500,000. If people are, indeed, risk-averse (and a flourishing insurance industry suggests that they are), rational individuals will want to allocate their scarce resources to minimize risk as well as to maximize wealth.

In many situations rational individuals can allocate society's scarce resources efficiently without need for government intervention. This occurs through the medium of voluntary exchange. Suppose John has baseball tickets he values at $5 while Jane has no tickets but would be willing to pay $10 to get some. Unless some obstacle prevents John and Jane from bargaining together, they will likely agree that John will sell the tickets to Jane in exchange for some payment between $5 and $10. Such a voluntary exchange is efficient under both the Pareto criteria (at least one person is made better off and no one is made worse off) and the Kaldor-Hicks or wealth maximization test (the tickets go to the person who values them most highly, as measured by willingness to pay compensation). Where the self-interested exchange behavior of rational individuals allocates resources to those who value them most, free markets are efficient.

In some cases, however, individuals' self-interested, rational maximizing behavior can lead to inefficient resource allocations that reduce society's utility and wealth. This occurs when individuals' choices involve *externalities*—costs or benefits to others. For example, a manufacturer may have to choose between an inexpensive manufacturing technology that imposes $100 in pollution costs on the manufacturer's neighbors, and a more sophisticated technology that benefits the neighbors by eliminating pollution but costs the manufacturer $20 more. Because others' costs and benefits are external to the self-interested rational maximizer's decision which technology to employ, the manufacturer may impose $100 in pollution costs on his neighbors rather than spend $20 himself. Thus rational individuals may pursue their own interests by inefficiently imposing greater harms on (or withholding greater benefits from) others.

When externalities go uncontrolled, society may not allocate its scarce resources efficiently. Legal rules that prevent individuals from imposing externalities on each other can allow a community to reach a higher level of happiness or utility than would be possible without such rules. That insight provides the foundation for the economic analysis of law in general, and of Constitutional law in particular.

THE ECONOMICS OF CONSTITUTIONAL LAW AND PUBLIC CHOICE

Economic analysis is usually associated with markets, which allocate resources through the voluntary actions of rational buyers and sellers exchanging goods and services. But not all goods are allocated through markets. Modern societies allocate many resources through political rather than market systems. Governments require auto manufacturers to install seatbelts and consumers to buy them, impose property, sales, and income taxes, provide police protection and public education, and pay farmers to keep agricultural land out of production. The government giveth and the government taketh away.

The tools of economics—the assumptions of utility maximization and rational choice—can be applied to political allocations as well as market allocations. The emerging discipline of "public choice" studies political decisionmaking through just such an economic lens. Among the questions public choice addresses are: why might rational individuals choose to have a political state? What sort of state and what sort of constitution are they likely to choose? How will individual preferences be translated into group preferences and social choices? And how can a government made up of egoistic, rational maximizing individuals pursue such group goals? The following materials examine these and other questions.

A. THEORY OF THE STATE

1. AN INTRODUCTION TO THE SOCIAL CONTRACT

Economists assume that rational maximizers voluntarily exchange resources in market transactions because exchange leaves both parties better off. Thus, market reallocations increase society's overall level of well-being. The efficiency of government allocations is more questionable. When the state requires a promisor to pay damages for breach of contract, imprisons a mugger for criminal assault, or requires a monopolist to charge competitive prices, the objects of such government coercion clearly are less well off than they would have been had the state not interfered. Nevertheless, there are reasons why rational maximizers might prefer a coercive state to the absence of government authority.

T. HOBBES, LEVIATHAN

(1651).

* * *

Hereby it is manifest, that during the time men live without a common power to keep them all in awe, they are in that condition which is called war; and such a war, as is of every man, against every man. * * *

* * * In such condition, there is no place for industry; because the fruit thereof is uncertain: and consequently no culture of the earth; no navigation, nor use of the commodities that may be imported by sea; no commodious building; no instruments of moving, and removing such things as require much force; no knowledge of the face of the earth; no account of time; no arts; no letters; no society; and which is worst of all, continual fear, and danger of violent death; and the life of man, solitary, poor, nasty, brutish, and short.

* * *

The final cause, end, or design of men (who naturally love liberty, and dominion over others) in the introduction of that restraint upon themselves (in which we see them live in commonwealths) is the foresight of their own preservation, and of a more contented life thereby; that is to say, of getting themselves out from that miserable condition of war, which is necessarily consequent * * * to the natural passions of men, when there is no visible power to keep them in awe, and tie them by fear of punishment to the performance of their covenants * * *.

For * * * covenants, without the sword, are but words, and of no strength to secure a man at all. * * *

* * *

* * * [T]herefore it is no wonder if there be somewhat else required (besides covenant) to make their agreement constant and lasting; which is a common power, to keep them in awe, and to direct their actions to the common benefit.

The only way to erect such a common power, as may be able to defend them from the invasion of foreigners, and the injuries of one another, and thereby to secure them in such sort, as that by their own industry, and by the fruits of the earth, they may nourish themselves and live contentedly; is, to confer all their power and strength upon one man, or upon one assembly of men, that may reduce all their wills, by plurality of voices, unto one will * * * and therein to submit their wills, every one to his will, and their judgments, to his judgment. This is more than consent, or concord; it is a real unity of them all, in one and the same person, made by covenant of every man with every man, in such manner, as if every man should say to every man, *I authorize and give up my right of governing myself, to this man, or to this* *assembly of men, on this condition, that thou give up thy right to him, and authorize all his actions in like manner.* This done, the multitude so united in one person, is called a COMMONWEALTH, in latin CIVITAS. This is the generation of that great LEVIATHAN, or rather (to speak more reverently) of that *mortal God,* to which we owe under the *immortal God,* our peace and defence. For by this authority, given him by every particular man in the commonwealth, he hath the use of so much power and strength conferred on him, that by terror thereof, he is enabled to perform the wills of them all, to peace at home, and mutual aid against their enemies abroad. And in him consisteth the essence of the commonwealth; which (to define it) is *one person, of whose acts a great multitude, by mutual covenants one with another, have made themselves every one the author, to the end he may use the strength and means of them all, as he shall think expedient, for their peace and common defence.*

And he that carrieth this person, is called SOVEREIGN, and said to have *sovereign power;* and every one besides, his SUBJECT.

* * *

JACOBSON v. COMMONWEALTH OF MASSACHUSETTS

Supreme Court of the United States, 1905.
197 U.S. 11, 25 S.Ct. 358, 49 L.Ed. 643.

HARLAN, JUSTICE.

This case involves the validity, under the Constitution of the United States, of certain provisions in the statutes of Massachusetts relating to vaccination.

* * *

* * * [T]he plaintiff in error, Jacobson, was proceeded against by a criminal complaint in one of the inferior courts of Massachusetts. The complaint charged that on the seventeenth day of July, 1902, the Board of Health of Cambridge, being of the opinion that it was necessary for the public health and safety, required the vaccination and revaccination of all the inhabitants thereof who had not been successfully vaccinated since the first day of March, 1897, and provided them with the means of free vaccination, and that the defendant, being over twenty-one years of age and not under guardianship, refused and neglected to comply with such requirement.

* * *

* * * [F]or nearly a century most of the members of the medical profession have regarded vaccination, repeated after intervals, as a preventive of smallpox; that while they have recognized the possibility of injury to an individual from carelessness in the performance of it, or even in a conceivable case without carelessness, they generally have considered the risk of such an injury too small to be seriously weighed

as against the benefits coming from the discreet and proper use of the preventive * * *.

* * *

The authority of the State to enact this statute is to be referred to what is commonly called the police power * * *. According to settled principles the police power of a State must be held to embrace, at least, such reasonable regulations established directly by legislative enactment as will protect the public health and the public safety. * * * The mode or manner in which those results are to be accomplished is within the discretion of the State, subject, of course, so far as Federal power is concerned, only to the condition that no rule prescribed by a State, nor any regulation adopted by a local governmental agency acting under the sanction of state legislation, shall contravene the Constitution of the United States, or infringe any right granted or secured by that instrument. * * *

We come, then, to inquire whether any right given, or secured by the Constitution, is invaded by the statute as interpreted by the state court. The defendant insists that his liberty is invaded when the State subjects him to fine or imprisonment for neglecting or refusing to submit to vaccination; that a compulsory vaccination law is unreasonable, arbitrary, and oppressive, and, therefore, hostile to the inherent right of every freeman to care for his own body and health in such way as to him seems best; and that the execution of such a law against one who objects to vaccination, no matter for what reason, is nothing short of an assault upon his person. But the liberty secured by the Constitution of the United States to every person within its jurisdiction does not import an absolute right in each person to be, at all times and in all circumstances, wholly freed from restraint. There are manifold restraints to which every person is necessarily subject for the common good. On any other basis organized society could not exist with safety to its members. Society based on the rule that each one is a law unto himself would soon be confronted with disorder and anarchy. Real liberty for all could not exist under the operation of a principle which recognizes the right of each individual person to use his own, whether in respect of his person or his property, regardless of the injury that may be done to others. * * * In the constitution of Massachusetts adopted in 1780 it was laid down as a fundamental principle of the social compact that the whole people covenants with each citizen, and each citizen with the whole people, that all shall be governed by certain laws for "the common good," and that government is instituted "for the common good, for the protection, safety, prosperity and happiness of the people, and not for the profit, honor or private interests of any one man, family or class of men." The good and welfare of the Commonwealth, of which the legislature is primarily the judge, is the basis on which the police power rests in Massachusetts.

* * * If the mode adopted by the Commonwealth of Massachusetts for the protection of its local communities against smallpox proved to

be distressing, inconvenient or objectionable to some—if nothing more could be reasonably affirmed of the statute in question—the answer is that it was the duty of the constituted authorities primarily to keep in view the welfare, comfort and safety of the many, and not permit the interests of the many to be subordinated to the wishes or convenience of the few. There is, of course, a sphere within which the individual may assert the supremacy of his own will and rightfully dispute the authority of any human government, especially of any free government existing under a written constitution, to interfere with the exercise of that will. But it is equally true that in every wellordered society charged with the duty of conserving the safety of its members the rights of the individual in respect of his liberty may at times, under the pressure of great dangers, be subjected to such restraint, to be enforced by reasonable regulations, as the safety of the general public may demand. * * * The liberty secured by the Fourteenth Amendment, this court has said, consists, in part, in the right of a person "to live and work where he will", and yet he may be compelled, by force if need be, against his will and without regard to his personal wishes or his pecuniary interests, or even his religious or political convictions, to take his place in the ranks of the army of his country and risk the chance of being shot down in its defense. It is not, therefore, true that the power of the public to guard itself against imminent danger depends in every case involving the control of one's body upon his willingness to submit to reasonable regulations established by the constituted authorities, under the sanction of the State, for the purpose of protecting the public collectively against such danger.

* * *

We are not prepared to hold that a minority, residing or remaining in any city or town where smallpox is prevalent, and enjoying the general protection afforded by an organized local government, may thus defy the will of its constituted authorities, acting in good faith for all, under the legislative sanction of the State. If such be the privilege of a minority then a like privilege would belong to each individual of the community, and the spectacle would be presented of the welfare and safety of an entire population being subordinated to the notions of a single individual who chooses to remain a part of that population. We are unwilling to hold it to be an element in the liberty secured by the Constitution of the United States that one person, or a minority of persons, residing in any community and enjoying the benefits of its local government, should have the power thus to dominate the majority when supported in their action by the authority of the State. * * *

* * *

The judgment of the court below must be affirmed.

It is so ordered.

Notes and Questions

1. In *Jacobson,* the Supreme Court held that Massachusetts could require an individual to submit to smallpox vaccination against his will.

Jacobson claimed that vaccination was likely to harm him because "he had suffered seriously from previous vaccination, thus indicating that his system was sensitive to the poison of the vaccination virus." 197 U.S. at 17, 25 S.Ct. at 359. The Supreme Court pointed out that it was within the state's police power not only to force Jacobson to submit to vaccination, but to require him to serve in the military and face the risk of death or crippling injury. *Jacobson*'s discussion of the limits of the police power serves as a reminder that the law is a system of behavioral rules that individuals follow not because they choose to, but because the human agents of an amorphous "commonwealth" compel them to. Behind every legal judgment lies the coercive power of the state.

> *Questions:* When the state forces an individual to do something she would rather not do, or prohibits her from doing something she would like to do, by definition the coerced individual suffers a loss of utility as a result of the government's interference. Does that mean government coercion is inefficient? Consider the facts of *Jacobson,* and assume that while smallpox vaccination poses a small risk to the vaccinated individual, a vaccinated person cannot transmit the disease to anyone else and complete vaccination of a population will eradicate the disease. Why might a rational individual like Jacobson refuse immunization? If there were no immunization requirement, would the risk of a smallpox epidemic likely increase or decrease? Was the compulsory vaccination statute involved in *Jacobson* inefficient?

2. Writing centuries apart, Harlan and Hobbes describe a contractual relationship between the individual and the state. Entering the "covenant of every man with every man," rational persons voluntarily agree to submit to government coercion in return for government protection. The notion of the "social contract" has proven one of the most powerful and persistent ideas in political theory and is reflected in both the classic writings of Hobbes, Locke, and Rousseau and the modern work of Kant, Nozick, and Rawls.

A rational maximizer will choose to enter a social contract only if doing so increases her level of well-being. That implies that a social contract, like other exchanges, is efficient. However, most discussion of contractarian theory has focused on its moral rather than its economic implications.

> *Questions:* How does the notion of a social contract provide a moral justification for intrusive state action? Why might Massachusetts claim that requiring Jacobson to submit to vaccination was not only within its legal authority but also within its moral authority?

3. While citing contractarian theory, Justice Harlan also argued that Cambridge's compulsory vaccination program was justified because "it was the duty of the constituted authorities primarily to keep in view the welfare, comfort, and safety of the many, and not permit the interests of the many to be subordinated to the wishes or convenience of the few."

> *Questions:* Compare the contractarian and "public welfare" justifications for the coercive state. Which more closely resembles Pareto's perspective? Which reflects the Kaldor–Hicks criteria?

4. Thomas Hobbes argued in *Leviathan* that state compulsion was essential to rein in individuals' "natural passions," which if uncontrolled would lead to a state of nature in which man's life was "nasty, brutish, and short." Justice Harlan similarly believed that a "[s]ociety based on the rule that each one is a law unto himself would soon be confronted with disorder and anarchy." Such statements imply that without a coercive government, individuals will impose external costs on and withhold external benefits from each other to an intolerable degree.

> *Questions:* Is the state of nature necessarily as unpleasant as Hobbes and Harlan imply? Using the facts of *Jacobson,* suppose there were no coercive state to require immunization. Could Cambridge's residents reach a voluntary, informal agreement to submit to a vaccination program? (Recall Hobbes' view that "covenants, without the sword, are but words, and of no strength to secure a man at all.") In the absence of state intervention or informal agreement, would a smallpox epidemic necessarily ensue? Consider whether there might be circumstances under Jacobson might voluntarily seek vaccination.

5. The *Jacobson* opinion concludes that "[w]e are not prepared to hold that a minority, residing or *remaining* in any city or town where smallpox is prevalent, and enjoying the general protection afforded by an organized local government, may thus defy the will of its constituted authorities" (emphasis added). That language raises the possibility that Jacobson might have escaped vaccination by simply moving away from Cambridge and settling in some other town that did not have a vaccination requirement.

> *Question:* Given that many factors may influence an individual's opinion of Cambridge's desirability as a place to live, does Jacobson's decision to remain in Cambridge say anything about the efficiency of the Cambridge statute?

PEREZ v. BROWNELL

Supreme Court of the United States, 1958.
356 U.S. 44, 78 S.Ct. 568, 2 L.Ed.2d 603.

FRANKFURTER, JUSTICE.

Petitioner, a national of the United States by birth, has been declared to have lost his American citizenship by operation of the Nationality Act of 1940 * * *. Section 401 of that Act provided that

> "A person who is a national of the United States, whether by birth or naturalization, shall lose his nationality by:
>
> "(e) Voting in a political election in a foreign state or participating in an election or plebiscite to determine the sovereignty over foreign territory * * *."

Petitioner was born in Texas in 1909. He resided in the United States until 1919 or 1920, when he moved with his parents to Mexico, where he lived, apparently without interruption, until 1943. * * *

Petitioner brought suit in 1954 in a United States District Court for a judgment declaring him to be a national of the United States. The court, sitting without a jury, found * * * that he had voted in a "political election" in Mexico in 1946. The court, concluding that he had thereby expatriated himself, denied the relief sought by the petitioner. The United States Court of Appeals for the Ninth Circuit affirmed. We granted certiorari because of the constitutional questions raised by the petitioner.

* * *

It cannot be said * * * that Congress acted without warrant when, pursuant to its power to regulate the relations of the United States with foreign countries, it provided that anyone who votes in a foreign election of significance politically in the life of another country shall lose his American citizenship. To deny the power of Congress to enact the legislation challenged here would be to disregard the constitutional allocation of governmental functions that it is this Court's solemn duty to guard.

* * *

Judgment affirmed.

WARREN, CHIEF JUSTICE, dissenting.

The Congress of the United States has decreed that a citizen of the United States shall lose his citizenship by performing certain designated acts. The petitioner in this case, a native-born American, is declared to have lost his citizenship by voting in a foreign election. Whether this forfeiture of citizenship exceeds the bounds of the Constitution is the issue before us. The problem is fundamental and must be resolved upon fundamental considerations.

Generally, when congressional action is challenged, constitutional authority is found in the express and implied powers with which the National Government has been invested or in those inherent powers that are necessary attributes of a sovereign state. The sweep of those powers is surely broad. In appropriate circumstances, they are adequate to take away life itself. The initial question here is whether citizenship is subject to the exercise of these general powers of government.

What is this government, whose power is here being asserted? And what is the source of that power? The answers are the foundation of our Republic. To secure the inalienable rights of the individual, "Governments are instituted among Men, deriving their just powers from the consent of the governed." I do not believe the passage of time has lessened the truth of this proposition. It is basic to our form of government. This Government was born of its citizens, it maintains itself in a continuing relationship with them, and, in my judgment, it is without power to sever the relationship that gives rise to its existence. I cannot believe that a government conceived in the spirit of ours was established with power to take from the people their most basic right.

Citizenship is man's basic right for it is nothing less than the right to have rights. Remove this priceless possession and there remains a stateless person, disgraced and degraded in the eyes of his countrymen. He has no lawful claim to protection from any nation, and no nation may assert rights on his behalf. * * * This government was not established with power to decree this fate.

* * *

There is no question that citizenship may be voluntarily relinquished. * * *

* * *

The fatal defect in the statute before us is that its application is not limited to those situations that may rationally be said to constitute an abandonment of citizenship. In specifying that any act of voting in a foreign political election results in loss of citizenship, Congress has employed a classification so broad that it encompasses conduct that fails to show a voluntary abandonment of American citizenship. * * *

* * * If the Government determines that certain conduct by United States citizens should be prohibited because of anticipated injurious consequences to the conduct of foreign affairs or to some other legitimate governmental interest, it may within the limits of the Constitution proscribe such activity and assess appropriate punishment. But every exercise of governmental power must find its source in the Constitution. The power to denationalize is not within the letter or the spirit of the powers with which our Government was endowed. The citizen may elect to renounce his citizenship, and under some circumstances he may be found to have abandoned his status by voluntarily performing acts that compromise his undivided allegiance to his country. The mere act of voting in a foreign election, however, without regard to the circumstances attending the participation, is not sufficient to show a voluntary abandonment of citizenship. The record in this case does not disclose any of the circumstances under which this petitioner voted. We know only the bare fact that he cast a ballot. The basic right of American citizenship has been too dearly won to be so lightly lost.

* * * As I see my duty in this case, I must dissent.

Notes and Questions

Like Justice Harlan's opinion in *Jacobson,* Chief Justice Warren's dissent in *Perez* refers to the "consent" theory of government—the notion that a state may legitimately coerce its citizens because they have consented, implicitly or explicitly, to that coercion. Justice Warren's emphasis on consent theory was so strong that he argued that implicit consent is necessary not only to bring an individual within the shadow of the state but also to expel him from it.

Questions: An individual's decision to remain within a particular jurisdiction may be evidence that she has consented to that jurisdiction's laws, presumably because she expects to be better off under those laws than she would be in another jurisdiction with a different social contract. Of course, one's ability to contract depends on several factors, including the existence of other parties interested in contracting and the costs of contracting. Do these considerations undermine the notion of implied consent as a justification for state coercion? Is consent a more plausible argument in *Perez,* which involved a "choice" of nationality, or in *Jacobson,* which involved a "choice" of municipal residence?

2. GOALS OF THE SOCIAL CONTRACT

Economic analysis explains why rational individuals might prefer a coercive government authority over the freedom of the "state of nature." Rational maximizers in the state of nature impose external costs on and withhold external benefits from each other in a wasteful, inefficient fashion that prevents society from reaching the much higher level of well-being possible when a government controls externalities. By mutually agreeing to submit to a coercive state, individuals force themselves to behave more responsibly and efficiently, improving the well-being of all.

The theory of the social contract may be more accurately described as a normative statement of the basis for an efficient and legitimate government than a positive description of the state's origins. Nevertheless, the idea has proven to be powerful and enduring. More than three centuries after Thomas Hobbes published *Leviathan,* Chief Justice Warren still regarded "government by the consent of the governed" as the foundation of the state's authority.

To suggest that rational individuals can improve their well-being by creating a political state only begins the inquiry into the notion of constitution as contract. Although many possible political states might be preferable to none, rational individuals would prefer some governments over others. The remainder of Chapter 7 considers how rational individuals might fashion the constitution for a coercive state—*i.e.,* draft the terms for the social contract. This section begins with the fundamental issue of what goal rational maximizers would want the social contract to serve.

a. Utilitarianism

If individuals prefer a coercive political state over the state of nature because they expect to be made better off, it seems natural that they should also prefer the political structure that makes them *best* off, *i.e.,* provides the most utility. Extrapolating from the principle of individual utility maximization leads naturally to *utilitarianism*—the notion that the social contract should seek the greatest happiness for the greatest number.

J. BENTHAM, AN INTRODUCTION TO THE PRINCIPLES OF MORALS AND LEGISLATION

(1832 ed.).

* * *

The principle of utility is the foundation of the present work: it will be proper therefore at the outset to give an explicit and determinate account of what is meant by it. By the principle of utility is meant that principle which approves or disapproves of every action whatsoever, according to the tendency which it appears to have to augment or diminish the happiness of the party whose interest is in question * * * .

* * *

The interest of the community is one of the most general expressions that can occur in the phraseology of morals: no wonder that the meaning of it is often lost. When it has a meaning, it is this. The community is a fictitious *body,* composed of the individual persons who are considered as constituting as it were its *members.* The interest of the community then is, what?—the sum of the interests of the several members who compose it.

* * *

An action then may be said to be conformable to the principle of utility, or, for shortness sake, to utility, (meaning with respect to the community at large) when the tendency it has to augment the happiness of the community is greater than any it has to diminish it.

* * *

Pleasures then, and the avoidance of pains, are the *ends* which the legislator has in view: it behoves him therefore to understand their *value.* * * *

* * *

To take an exact account then of the general tendency of any act, by which the interests of a community are affected, proceed as follows. Begin with any one person of those whose interests seem most immediately to be affected by it * * *.

* * *

Sum up all the values of all the *pleasures* on the one side, and those of all the *pains* on the other. The balance, if it be on the side of pleasure, will give the *good* tendency of the act upon the whole, with respect to the interests of that *individual* person; if on the side of pain, the *bad* tendency of it upon the whole.

Take an account of the *number* of persons whose interests appear to be concerned; and repeat the above process with respect to each.

Sum up the numbers expressive of the degrees of *good* tendency, which the act has, with respect to each individual, in regard to whom the tendency of it is *good* upon the whole: do this again with respect to each individual, in regard to whom the tendency of it is *bad* upon the whole. Take the *balance;* which, if on the side of *pleasure,* will give the general *good tendency* of the act, with respect to the total number of community of individuals concerned; if on the side of pain, the general *evil tendency,* with respect to the same community.

* * *

The end of law is, to augment happiness. The general object which all laws have, or ought to have, in common, is to augment the total happiness of the community * * * .

Notes and Questions

1. Since at least Bentham's day, the idea that the state's sole purpose should be maximizing its citizens' utility has sparked a heated and enduring debate. See generally J. Smart & B. Williams, Utilitarianism: For and Against (1973).

Questions: How does utilitarian theory compare with religious or ethical theories of the state? Is Marxism or Islamic fundamentalism consistent with utilitarianism?

2. Bentham argued that total happiness should be calculated by adding together the utilities and disutilities of all the individual members of society.

Question: How do the goals of a utilitarian state, as described by Bentham, relate to the economic goals of Pareto optimality and wealth maximization under the Kaldor–Hicks criteria?

To the economist concerned with efficiently maximizing utility, utilitarian theory has obvious attractions. However, a truly utilitarian society might adopt legal rules that many find troubling. The following cases explore some of the less-attractive aspects of utilitarianism.

BOWERS v. HARDWICK

Supreme Court of the United States, 1986.
478 U.S. 186, 106 S.Ct. 2841, 92 L.Ed.2d 140.

WHITE, JUSTICE.

In August 1982, respondent Hardwick was charged with violating the Georgia statute criminalizing sodomy by committing that act with another adult male in the bedroom of respondent's home. After a preliminary hearing, the District Attorney decided not to present the matter to the grand jury unless further evidence developed.

Respondent then brought suit in the Federal District Court, challenging the constitutionality of the statute insofar as it criminalized consensual sodomy. * * *

* * *

This case does not require a judgment on whether laws against sodomy between consenting adults in general, or between homosexuals in particular, are wise or desirable. * * * The issue presented is whether the Federal Constitution confers a fundamental right upon homosexuals to engage in sodomy and hence invalidates the laws of the many States that still make such conduct illegal and have done so for a very long time. * * *

* * *

Respondent * * * relies on *Stanley v. Georgia,* where the Court held that the First Amendment prevents conviction for possessing and reading obscene material in the privacy of his home: "If the First Amendment means anything, it means that a State has no business telling a man, sitting alone in his house, what books he may read or what films he may watch."

Stanley did protect conduct that would not have been protected outside the home, and it partially prevented the enforcement of state obscenity laws; but the decision was firmly grounded in the First Amendment. The right pressed upon us here has no similar support in the text of the Constitution, and it does not qualify for recognition under the prevailing principles for construing the Fourteenth Amendment. * * *

Even if the conduct at issue here is not a fundamental right, respondent asserts that there must be a rational basis for the law and that there is none in this case other than the presumed belief of a majority of the electorate in Georgia that homosexual sodomy is immoral and unacceptable. This is said to be an inadequate rationale to support the law. The law, however, is constantly based on notions of morality, and if all laws representing essentially moral choices are to be invalidated under the Due Process Clause, the courts will be very busy indeed. Even respondent makes no such claim, but insists that majority sentiments about the morality of homosexuality should be declared inadequate. We do not agree, and are unpersuaded that the sodomy laws of some 25 States should be invalidated on this basis.

Accordingly, the judgment of the Court of Appeals is reversed.

BURGER, CHIEF JUSTICE, concurring.

I join the Court's opinion, but I write separately to underscore my view that in constitutional terms there is no such thing as a fundamental right to commit homosexual sodomy.

* * * Decisions of individuals relating to homosexual conduct have been subject to state intervention throughout the history of Western Civilization. Condemnation of those practices is firmly rooted in Judeo-Christian moral and ethical standards. Homosexual sodomy was a capital crime under Roman law. During the English Reformation when powers of the ecclesiastical courts were transferred to the King's Courts, the first English statute criminalizing sodomy was passed.

Blackstone described "the infamous *crime against nature* " as an offense of "deeper malignity" than rape, an heinous act "the very mention of which is a disgrace to human nature," and "a crime not fit to be named." The common law of England, including its prohibition of sodomy, became the received law of Georgia and the other Colonies. In 1816 the Georgia Legislature passed the statute at issue here, and that statute has been continuously in force in one form or another since that time. To hold that the act of homosexual sodomy is somehow protected as a fundamental right would be to cast aside millennia of moral teaching.

This is essentially not a question of personal "preferences" but rather of the legislative authority of the State. I find nothing in the Constitution depriving a State of the power to enact the statute challenged here.

BLACKMUN, JUSTICE, dissenting.

This case is no more about "a fundamental right to engage in homosexual sodomy," as the Court purports to declare, than *Stanley v. Georgia* was about a fundamental right to watch obscene movies * * *. Rather, this case is about "the most comprehensive of rights and the right most valued by civilized men," namely, "the right to be let alone."

* * *

In a variety of circumstances we have recognized that a necessary corollary of giving individuals freedom to choose how to conduct their lives is acceptance of the fact that different individuals will make different choices. For example, in holding that the clearly important state interest in public education should give way to a competing claim by the Amish to the effect that extended formal schooling threatened their way of life, the Court declared: "There can be no assumption that today's majority is 'right' and the Amish and others like them are 'wrong.' A way of life that is odd or even erratic but interferes with no rights or interests of others is not to be condemned because it is different." The Court claims that its decision today merely refuses to recognize a fundamental right to engage in homosexual sodomy; what the Court really has refused to recognize is the fundamental interest all individuals have in controlling the nature of their intimate associations with others.

* * *

The Court's failure to comprehend the magnitude of the liberty interests at stake in this case leads it to slight the question whether petitioner, on behalf of the State, has justified Georgia's infringement on these interests. * * *

* * *

The core of petitioner's defense of § 16–6–2 * * * is that respondent and others who engage in the conduct prohibited by § 16–6–2 interfere with Georgia's exercise of the " 'right of the Nation and of the States to maintain a decent society.' " Essentially, petitioner argues, and the Court agrees, that the fact that the acts described in § 16–6–2 "for hundreds of years, if not thousands, have been uniformly condemned as immoral" is a sufficient reason to permit a State to ban them today.

I cannot agree that either the length of time a majority has held its convictions or the passions with which it defends them can withdraw legislation from this Court's scrutiny. * * * [B]ecause the issue raised by this case touches the heart of what makes individuals what they are * * * we should be especially sensitive to the rights of those whose choices upset the majority.

* * *

Nor can § 16–6–2 be justified as a "morally neutral" exercise of Georgia's power to "protect the public environment". Certainly, some private behavior can affect the fabric of society as a whole. * * * [But p]etitioner and the Court fail to see the difference between laws that protect public sensibilities and those that enforce private morality. Statutes banning public sexual activity are entirely consistent with protecting the individual's liberty interest in decisions concerning sexual relations: the same recognition that those decisions are intensely private which justifies protecting them from governmental interference can justify protecting individuals from unwilling exposure to the sexual activities of others. But the mere fact that intimate behavior may be punished when it takes place in public cannot dictate how States can regulate intimate behavior that occurs in intimate places.

This case involves no real interference with the rights of others, for the mere knowledge that other individuals do not adhere to one's value system cannot be a legally cognizable interest, let alone an interest that can justify invading the houses, hearts, and minds of citizens who choose to live their lives differently.

* * *

* * * I can only hope that * * * the Court soon will reconsider its analysis and conclude that depriving individuals of the right to choose for themselves how to conduct their intimate relationships poses a far greater threat to the values most deeply rooted in our Nation's history than tolerance of nonconformity could ever do. Because I think the Court today betrays those values, I dissent.

Notes and Questions

1. The Georgia statute challenged in *Bowers* provides that "[a] person commits the offense of sodomy when he performs or submits to any sexual act involving the sex organs of one person and the mouth or anus of another." The statute's language is not limited to homosexual conduct but appears to extend to consensual sex between married, heterosexual partners. The punishment for conviction of a single offense is "imprisonment for not less than one nor more than 20 years." Ga. Code Ann. § 16–6–2 (1984).

2. The State of Georgia's justification for its antisodomy statute, accepted by the Supreme Court, was the "presumed belief of a majority of the electorate in Georgia that homosexual sodomy is immoral and unacceptable." A utilitarian would agree that the majority's notions of morality are a legitimate justification for regulating conduct, even if that conduct does not affect others directly. If the "moral majority's" utility from prohibiting offensive and immoral conduct outweighs the disutility suffered by those who would prefer to engage in immoral acts, morality statutes are utility maximizing.

The idea that A's notions of morality justify regulating B's private conduct is in tension with the libertarian (or, as it is sometimes called, liberal) view that individual dignity and autonomy demand there be some areas where others' preferences are irrelevant to the individual's decision how to conduct herself. John Stuart Mill was one of the leading proponents of that view, J.S. Mill, On Liberty 552 (Dolphin ed. 1961) (first publication 1859):

> What, then, is the rightful limit to the sovereignty of the individual over himself? Where does the authority of society begin? * * *
>
> * * *
>
> * * * As soon as any part of a person's conduct affects prejudicially the interests of others, society has jurisdiction over it, and the question whether the general welfare will or will not be promoted by interfering with it, becomes open to discussion. But there is no room for entertaining any such question when a person's conduct affects the interests of no persons besides himself, or need not affect them unless they like (all the persons concerned being of full age, and the ordinary amount of understanding). In all such cases, there should be perfect freedom, legal and social, to do the action and stand the consequences.

In Jacobson v. Massachusetts, above, Justice Harlan expressed a similar view that "[t]here is, of course, a sphere within which the individual may assert the supremacy of his own will and rightfully dispute the authority of any human government."

> *Question:* Justice Blackmun's dissent in *Bowers* differentiated between laws protecting "public sensibilities" and laws enforcing "private morality." Mills also distinguished between conduct that prejudiced others' interests and conduct that need not affect others "unless they like," *i.e.,* unless they allowed themselves to be affected. Does utilitarianism provide any basis for Blackmun's and Mill's distinctions?

3. Amartya Sen has provided a proof of the conflict between liberal values and utility maximization using the following example. Mr. Lewd and Mr. Prude share a single copy of D.H. Lawrence's Lady Chatterley's Lover. Mr. Prude prefers that no one reads the book, but if it must be read, he would rather endure reading it himself than allow Mr. Lewd to wallow in such filth. Mr. Lewd would prefer that they both read the book, but if only one can read it he would give up the pleasure of reading it himself for the glee of knowing that Mr. Prude must read it. The optimal result from the point of utility maximization is that Mr. Prude reads Lady Chatterley's Lover while Mr. Lewd does not. Yet that is exactly the

opposite of what the liberal value system says should occur, *i.e.,* each should make his own decision to read the book or not while ignoring the other's decision—in which case Mr. Lewd will read the book and Mr. Prude won't. See A. K. Sen, Collective Choice and Social Welfare 79–88 (1970).

The conflict between utility maximization and liberalism arises from Mr. Lewd and Mr. Prude both having "nosy" preferences; each experiences utility and disutility from the other's private behavior. Sen suggests one way out of the "liberal paradox" is for Mr. Lewd and Mr. Prude to impose upon themselves liberal values and to ignore their preferences relating to others' private behavior.

Question: Is Sen's solution to the liberal paradox consistent with utilitarianism?

4. In *Bowers,* the Supreme Court refused to find the sexual conduct prohibited by the Georgia statute to be constitutionally protected. However, in other cases the Court has recognized an individual's fundamental right to privacy and applied strict scrutiny to strike down, under Due Process or Equal Protection theories, statutes regulating individuals' choices in "private" matters. See, e.g., Griswold v. Connecticut, 381 U.S. 479, 85 S.Ct. 1678, 14 L.Ed.2d 510 (1965) (right to use contraceptives); Roe v. Wade, 410 U.S. 113, 93 S.Ct. 705, 35 L.Ed.2d 147 (1973) (woman's right to abortion in first trimester); Cruzan v. Director, Missouri Department of Health, 497 U.S. 261, 110 S.Ct. 2841, 111 L.Ed.2d 224 (1990) (implying vegetative patient's right to die rather than receive extraordinary medical care).

Question: Is a fundamental right to privacy inconsistent with utilitarianism and utility maximization?

KOREMATSU v. UNITED STATES

Supreme Court of the United States, 1944.
323 U.S. 214, 65 S.Ct. 193, 89 L.Ed. 194.

[The majority opinion in this "Japanese Internment Case" focused on the constitutional validity of a military order forbidding any United States citizen of Japanese descent to remain in certain areas of the Pacific coast. That order was part of an overall plan for the forced detention of Japanese–Americans in internment camps. Another military order, which the majority declined to review, prohibited Japanese–Americans from *leaving* the restricted zone. As Justice Roberts noted in his dissent in *Korematsu,* "[t]he predicament in which the petitioner [found] himself was this: He was forbidden, by Military Order, to leave the zone in which he lived; he was forbidden, by Military Order, after a date fixed, to be found within that zone unless he were in an Assembly Center located in that zone. General DeWitt's report to the Secretary of War concerning the programme of evacuation and relocation of Japanese makes it entirely clear * * * that an Assembly Center was a euphemism for a prison." 323 U.S. at 230.]

BLACK, JUSTICE.

The petitioner, an American citizen of Japanese descent, was convicted in a federal district court for remaining in San Leandro, California, a "Military Area," contrary to Civilian Exclusion Order No. 34 of the Commanding General of the Western Command, U.S. Army, which directed that after May 9, 1942, all persons of Japanese ancestry should be excluded from that area. No question was raised as to petitioner's loyalty to the United States. The Circuit Court of Appeals affirmed, and the importance of the constitutional question involved caused us to grant certiorari.

It should be noted, to begin with, that all legal restrictions which curtail the civil rights of a single racial group are immediately suspect. That is not to say that all such restrictions are unconstitutional. It is to say that courts must subject them to the most rigid scrutiny. * * *

* * *

* * * [W]e are unable to conclude that it was beyond the war power of Congress and the Executive to exclude those of Japanese ancestry from the West Coast war area at the time they did. True, exclusion from the area in which one's home is located is a [great] deprivation * * *. Nothing short of apprehension by the proper military authorities of the gravest imminent danger to the public safety can constitutionally justify [it]. But exclusion from a threatened area * * * has a definite and close relationship to the prevention of espionage and sabotage. The military authorities, charged with the primary responsibility of defending our shores, concluded that curfew provided inadequate protection and ordered exclusion. They did so * * * in accordance with Congressional authority to the military to say who should, and who should not, remain in the threatened areas.

* * *

We uphold the exclusion order as of the time it was made and when the petitioner violated it. In doing so, we are not unmindful of the hardships imposed by it upon a large group of American citizens. But hardships are part of war, and war is an aggregation of hardships. All citizens alike, both in and out of uniform, feel the impact of war in greater or lesser measure. Citizenship has its responsibilities as well as its privileges, and in time of war the burden is always heavier. Compulsory exclusion of large groups of citizens from their homes, except under circumstances of direst emergency and peril, is inconsistent with our basic governmental institutions. But when under conditions of modern warfare our shores are threatened by hostile forces, the power to protect must be commensurate with the threatened danger.

* * *

Affirmed.

JACKSON, JUSTICE, dissenting.

Korematsu was born on our soil, of parents born in Japan. The Constitution makes him a citizen of the United States by nativity and a citizen of California by residence. No claim is made that he is not loyal to this country. There is no suggestion that apart from the matter involved here he is not law-abiding and well disposed. Korematsu, however, has been convicted of an act not commonly a crime. It consists merely of being present in the state whereof he is a citizen, near the place where he was born, and where all his life he has lived.

* * *

Now, if any fundamental assumption underlies our system, it is that guilt is personal and not inheritable. * * * But here is an attempt to make an otherwise innocent act a crime merely because this prisoner is the son of parents as to whom he had no choice, and belongs to a race from which there is no way to resign. * * *

* * *

* * * I would reverse the judgment and discharge the prisoner.

Notes and Questions

1. The *Korematsu* decision makes it clear that the Constitution permits the government to impose severe deprivations upon innocent individuals when the public need is great enough. In *Korematsu,* the perceived threat was one to national security. The military authorities on the Pacific Coast believed that the uncontrolled movement of Japanese–Americans posed an unavoidable threat of sabotage that might be disastrous to the war effort. The Supreme Court accepted that argument and held that the perceived threat to the nation's security justified the effective imprisonment of all American citizens of Japanese descent living on the West Coast.

Utilitarian theory supports the *Korematsu* decision. A state action that prevents significant harm to the vast majority of society's members may maximize utility even though a small minority suffers greatly. As Justice Harlan noted in Jacobson v. Massachusetts, above, "[i]f the mode adopted by the Commonwealth of Massachusetts for the protection of its local communities against smallpox proved to be distressing, inconvenient or objectionable to some * * * the answer is that it was the duty of the constituted authorities primarily to keep in view the welfare, comfort and safety of the many, and not permit the interests of the many to be subordinated to the wishes or convenience of the few."

2. There was some suggestion in *Korematsu* that the principal "benefit" West Coast residents derived from the Japanese–Americans' internment was not freedom from sabotage but the opportunity to acquire the internees' property at bargain prices and to eliminate Japanese–American competition in the marketplace. Justice Murphy also wrote a dissent in *Korematsu,* in which he noted that "[s]pecial interest groups were extremely active in applying pressure for mass evacuation. Mr. Austin E. Anson, managing secretary of the Salinas Vegetable Grower–Shipper Association, has frankly admitted that 'We're charged with wanting to get rid of the Japs for selfish reasons. We do. * * * They undersell the white man in the markets. * * * They work their women and children while the white farmer has to pay wages for his help. If all the Japs were removed tomorrow, we'd never miss them in two weeks, because the white farmers can take over and produce everything the Jap grows. And we don't want

them back when the war ends, either.' " 323 U.S. at 240 n.12, 65 S.Ct. at 205 n.12.

Under utilitarian theory such sentiments legitimately may be considered in calculating whether the harm state action imposes on the minority is outweighed by the benefit to the majority. Because all preferences are equally acceptable, any reallocation is justified if the calculus of utilities suggests total utility is increased. Taken to an extreme, utilitarian theory would allow a society to torture an innocent individual to entertain a large sadistic audience, provided the mob's total glee outweighed the victim's agony. Of course, that scenario is unlikely. The more realistic problem posed by utilitarian values is that utilitarianism allows social rules under which most individuals prosper, but a few live in wretched conditions.

b. Rawls' Theory of Justice

J. RAWLS, A THEORY OF JUSTICE *

(1971).

Justice is the first virtue of social institutions, as truth is of systems of thought. A theory however elegant and economical must be rejected or revised if it is untrue; likewise laws and institutions no matter how efficient and well-arranged must be reformed or abolished if they are unjust. Each person possesses an inviolability founded on justice that even the welfare of society as a whole cannot override. For this reason justice denies that the loss of freedom for some is made right by a greater good shared by others. It does not allow that the sacrifices imposed on a few are outweighed by the larger sum of advantages enjoyed by many.

* * *

My aim is to present a conception of justice which generalizes and carries to a higher level of abstraction the familiar theory of the social contract as found, say, in Locke, Rousseau, and Kant. In order to do this we are not to think of the original contract as one to enter a particular society or to set up a particular form of government. Rather, the guiding idea is that the principles of justice for the basic structure of society are the object of the original agreement. They are the principles that free and rational persons concerned to further their own interests would accept in an initial position of equality as defining the fundamental terms of their association. * * *

* * *

* * * No society can, of course, be a scheme of cooperation which men enter voluntarily in a literal sense; each person finds himself placed at birth in some particular position in some particular society, and the nature of this position materially affects his life prospects. Yet

a society satisfying the principles of justice * * * comes as close as a society can to being a voluntary scheme, for it meets the principles which free and equal persons would assent to under circumstances that are fair. In this sense its members are autonomous and the obligations they recognize self-imposed.

* * *

I shall maintain [that] the persons in the initial situation would choose two rather different principles: the first requires equality in the assignment of basic rights and duties, while the second holds that social and economic inequalities, for example inequalities of wealth and authority, are just only if they result in compensating benefits for everyone, and in particular for the least advantaged members of society. These principles rule out justifying institutions on the grounds that the hardships of some are offset by a greater good in the aggregate. It may be expedient but it is not just that some should have less in order that others may prosper. But there is no injustice in the greater benefits earned by a few provided that the situation of persons not so fortunate is thereby improved. The intuitive idea is that since everyone's well-being depends upon a scheme of cooperation without which no one could have a satisfactory life, the division of advantages should be such as to draw forth the willing cooperation of everyone taking part in it, including those less well situated. * * * The two principles mentioned seem to be fair agreement on the basis of which those better endowed, or more fortunate in their social position, neither of which we can be said to deserve, could expect the willing cooperation of others when some workable scheme is a necessary condition of the welfare of all. * * *

* * *

My aim is to work out a theory of justice that represents an alternative to utilitarian thought * * * that society is rightly ordered, and therefore just, when its major institutions are arranged so as to achieve the greatest net balance of satisfaction summed over all the individuals belonging to it.

* * *

* * * [T]he two principles read as follows.

> First: each person is to have an equal right to the most extensive basic liberty compatible with a similar liberty for others.
>
> Second: social and economic inequalities are to be arranged so that they are * * * reasonably expected to be to everyone's advantage * * *

* * * As their formulation suggests, these principles presuppose that the social structure can be divided into two more or less distinct parts, the first principle applying to the one, the second to the other. They distinguish between those aspects of the social system that define and secure the equal liberties of citizenship and those that specify and establish social and economic inequalities. The basic liberties of citizens are, roughly speaking, political liberty (the right to vote and to be

eligible for public office) together with freedom of speech and assembly; liberty of conscience and freedom of thought; freedom of the person along with the right to hold (personal) property; and freedom from arbitrary arrest and seizure as defined by the concept of the rule of law. These liberties are all required to be equal by the first principle, since citizens of a just society are to have the same basic rights.

The second principle applies, in the first approximation, to the distribution of income and wealth * * *. While the distribution of wealth and income need not be equal, it must be to everyone's advantage * * * One applies the second principle * * * [by arranging] social and economic inequalities so that everyone benefits.

* * *

* * * [I]t should be observed that the two principles (and this holds for all formulations) are a special case of a more general conception of justice that can be expressed as follows.

> All social values—liberty and opportunity, income and wealth, and bases of self-respect—are to be distributed equally unless an unequal distribution of any, or all, of these values is to everyone's advantage.

* * *

Thus, the parties start with a principle establishing equal liberty for all, including equality of opportunity, as well as an equal distribution of income and wealth. But there is no reason why this acknowledgment should be final. If there are inequalities in the basic structure that work to make everyone better off in comparison with the benchmark of initial equality, why not permit them? The immediate gain which a greater inequality might allow can be regarded as intelligently invested in view of its future return. If, for example, these inequalities set up various incentives which succeed in eliciting more productive efforts, a person in the original position may look upon them as necessary to cover the costs of training and to encourage effective performance. * * * A person in the original position would, therefore, concede the justice of these inequalities. Indeed it would be shortsighted of him not to do so. Inequalities are permissible when they maximize, or at least all contribute to the long-term expectations of the least fortunate group in society.

* * *

* * * [I]t is useful as a heuristic device to think of the two principles as the maximin solution to the problem of social justice. * * * The maximin rule tells us to rank alternatives by their worst possible outcomes: we are to adopt the alternative the worst outcome of which is superior to the worst outcomes of the others. * * *

Notes and Questions

1. Rawls' analysis is rooted firmly in the tradition of the social contract, yet he proposes contractual terms that differ significantly from traditional utilitarian theories. Rawls argues that rational individuals

drafting a social contract from "the original position" (a hypothetical condition corresponding to a state of nature in which no one knows what position he will occupy in society) would choose a society that distributes goods according to two principles of justice. The *equality principle* requires basic political freedoms and liberties to be distributed perfectly equally. The *difference principle* allows differences among individuals in the distribution of economic rights like wealth and income, but only so long as those differences improve the economic position of the worst-off in society.

Rawls describes both principles as an extension of the general rule that all social goods "are to be distributed equally unless an unequal distribution of any, or all, of these values is to everyone's advantage." That is Rawls' rule of "maximin;" inequalities are tolerated when they operate to *maximize* the rights of those who enjoy the *minimum* in society. Rawls argues that there is no reason to tolerate inequalities in basic political liberties because there is no way disparities in political liberties can increase the degree of political liberty enjoyed by those worst-off in society. On the other hand, he believes that allowing differences in wealth and power can improve the economic position of the least-advantaged.

Question: Rawls seems to assume that the supply of basic political liberties like voting rights is fixed, so that increasing one person's political liberty necessarily decreases another's. In contrast, Rawls presumes that the supply of economic wealth is not fixed and allowing inequality can increase total wealth in a fashion that benefits all the members of society. Are Rawls' technological assumptions about the supply of wealth and political liberties sensible?

2. Rawls describes his theory as a theory of "justice." Nevertheless, his analysis has an economic flavor.

Question: Rawls presents his theory as an alternative to utilitarianism. While utilitarians are concerned only with the total amount of utility in society and not with its distribution, Rawls' theory does not allow the interests of an individual to be sacrificed for the greater good. What is the relationship between utilitarianism and Rawls' theory as political ideas, and Kaldor–Hicks wealth maximization and the Pareto criteria as economic ideas?

UNIVERSAL DECLARATION OF HUMAN RIGHTS

General Assembly Resolution 217(III).
Dec. 10, 1948.

* * *

Article 25

1. Everyone has the right to a standard of living adequate for the health and well-being of himself and of his family, including food, clothing, housing and medical care and necessary social services, and the right to security in the event of unemployment, sickness, disability, widowhood, old age or other lack of livelihood in circumstances beyond his control.

* * *

Notes and Questions

1. As Bowers v. Hardwick, above, illustrates, the Supreme Court normally upholds state action if it is rationally related to some legitimate government purpose. The rational relation standard is easily met and statutes reviewed under that standard are rarely struck down. In cases involving "fundamental rights," however, the Court applies the more severe standard of strict scrutiny. Under the Due Process Clause, strict scrutiny requires that government action burdening a fundamental right be necessary to a compelling state objective. See Roe v. Wade, 410 U.S. 113, 93 S.Ct. 705, 35 L.Ed.2d 147 (1973). The Equal Protection Clause similarly requires classifications involving fundamental rights to be narrowly tailored to promote a compelling state interest. See Kramer v. Union Free School District, 395 U.S. 621, 89 S.Ct. 1886, 23 L.Ed.2d 583 (1969).

Which rights, then, are fundamental? The Supreme Court has held that the Constitution explicitly guarantees a number of political rights to U.S. citizens, including the rights to peaceable assembly, to free speech, and to trial by jury. The Court has found other fundamental rights implicit in the Constitution, including the rights to vote (under the Equal Protection clause) and to travel from state to state.

In Shapiro v. Thompson, 394 U.S. 618, 89 S.Ct. 1322, 22 L.Ed.2d 600 (1969), the Court struck down as unconstitutional state statutes that denied welfare assistance to residents who had not resided within a state's jurisdiction for at least one year prior to applying for assistance. The principal focus of Justice Brennan's opinion for the majority was the burden the statutes imposed upon the judicially-recognized fundamental right to interstate travel. However, Brennan also hinted that the residency requirements might be unconstitutional because the statutes precluded new residents from receiving "welfare aid upon which may depend the ability of the families to obtain the very means to subsist—food, shelter, and other necessities of life." 394 U.S. at 627, 89 S.Ct. at 1889. Justice Harlan's dissent in *Shapiro* protested Brennan's "cryptic suggestion" that strict scrutiny applied because the classification affected the appellees' access to food or shelter, 394 U.S. at 661–62, 89 S.Ct. at 1345–46:

> Virtually every state statute affects important rights. * * * When the right affected is one assured by the Federal Constitution, any infringement can be dealt with under the Due Process Clause. But when a statute affects only matters not mentioned in the Federal Constitution and is not arbitrary or irrational, I must reiterate that I know of nothing which entitles this Court to pick out particular human activities, characterize them as "fundamental," and give them added protection under an unusually stringent equal protection test.

Lindsey v. Normet, 405 U.S. 56, 92 S.Ct. 862, 31 L.Ed.2d 36 (1972), involved a challenge to procedural limitations imposed on tenants' suits against landlords under Oregon's Forcible Entry and Wrongful Detainer Law. The complainants urged the Court to examine the statute under a stricter standard than mere rationality review because the statute affected the poor's fundamental interest in shelter. Justice White's opinion for the Court instructed, 405 U.S. at 74, 92 S.Ct. at 874:

> We do not denigrate the importance of decent, safe and sanitary housing. But the Constitution does not provide judicial remedies for every social and economic ill. We are unable to perceive in that document any constitutional guarantee of access to dwellings of a particular quality. * * * Absent constitutional mandate, the assurance of adequate housing and the definition of landlord-tenant relationships are legislative, not judicial, functions.

Similarly, in Dandridge v. Williams, 397 U.S. 471, 90 S.Ct. 1153, 25 L.Ed.2d 491 (1970), the Court held that the fact that public welfare assistance affected the most basic economic needs of the poor did not justify strict scrutiny.

In San Antonio Independent School District v. Rodriguez, 411 U.S. 1, 93 S.Ct. 1278, 36 L.Ed.2d 16 (1973), it became clear that Harlan's view that the Constitution did not recognize fundamental economic rights to food, shelter or education had won out. *Rodriguez* was a class action brought on behalf of poor and minority children challenging Texas' system of financing public education. Powell's opinion for the majority admitted that education was essential to the individual's progress in life, including the ability to exercise political liberties, but nevertheless upheld the Texas system under a mere rationality standard, 411 U.S. at 33–37, 93 S.Ct. at 1296–99.

> It is not the province of this Court to create substantive constitutional rights in the name of guaranteeing equal protection of the laws. Thus, the key to discovering whether education is 'fundamental' is not to be found in comparisons of the relative societal significance of education as opposed to subsistence or housing. * * * Rather, the answer lies in assessing whether there is a right to education explicitly or implicitly guaranteed by the Constitution.
>
> Education, of course, is not among the rights afforded explicit protection under our Federal Constitution. Nor do we find any basis for saying it is implicitly so protected. * * * It is appellees' contention * * * that education is distinguishable from other services and benefits provided by the State because it bears a peculiarly close relationship to other rights and liberties accorded protection under the Constitution. Specifically, they insist that education is itself a fundamental personal right because it is essential to the effective exercise of First Amendment freedoms and to intelligent utilization of the right to vote. * * *
>
> * * *
>
> * * * [T]he logical limitations on appellees' nexus theory are difficult to perceive. How, for instance, is education to be distinguished from the significant personal interests in the basics of decent food and shelter? Empirical examination might well buttress an assumption that the ill-fed, ill-clothed, and ill-housed are among the most ineffective participants in the political process, and that they derive the least enjoyment from the benefits of the First Amendment. If so, appellees' thesis would cast serious doubt on the authority of *Dandridge v. Williams* and *Lindsey v. Normet.*

> We have carefully considered each of the arguments supportive of the District Court's finding that education is a fundamental right or liberty and have found those arguments unpersuasive. * * *

Shapiro and *Rodriguez* mark the rise and fall of the notion that the Constitution protects "economic" rights to a share of society's resources as well as political liberties. See also DeShaney v. Winnebago County Dept. of Social Services, 489 U.S. 189, 109 S.Ct. 998, 103 L.Ed.2d 249 (1989) ("[The Due Process Clause] is phrased as a limitation on the State's power to act, not as a guarantee of certain minimal levels of safety and security. * * * [O]ur cases have recognized that the Due Process Clauses generally confer no affirmative right to governmental aid, even where such aid may be necessary to secure life, liberty, or property interests.").

Questions: Compare the United States Supreme Court's view of entitlements to political and economic rights with the United Nation's aspirations in the *Declaration of Human Rights.* To what extent are the Supreme Court's and the United Nation's theories of rights consistent with Rawls' equality principle? With Rawls' difference principle?

2. In Rawls' "original position," individuals negotiate the social contract in ignorance of the role they are likely to play in their future society. They do not know if they are going to belong to the best-off or worst-off classes. Rawls believed rational persons choosing a social contract under such circumstances would choose to distribute social goods according to the maximin principle because (A Theory of Justice 154 (1971)):

> the person choosing * * * cares very little, if anything, for what he might gain above the minimum stipend that he can, in fact, be sure of by following the maximin rule. It is not worthwhile for him to take a chance for the sake of a further advantage, especially when it may turn out that he loses much that is important to him. * * * [T]he rejected alternatives have outcomes one can hardly accept. The situation involves grave risks.

Questions: What does Rawls assume about people's willingness to accept risk in the original position? Is that assumption realistic?

3. As Rawls himself admitted, "[c]learly the maximin rule is not, in general, a suitable guide for choices under uncertainty. * * * Offhand, the most natural rule of choice would seem to be to compute the expectation of monetary gain for each decision and then to adopt the course of action with the highest prospect." A Theory of Justice 153 (1971). A utilitarian society that does not care particularly about the worst-off in society but only about maximizing the sum of all its members' utility would probably adopt the second rule, which can be characterized as maximizing the individual's expected *average* utility.

Question: If persons drafting a social contract from Rawls' original position choose the principle of maximizing expected average utility, what does that imply about their attitudes towards risk?

4. The jurisprudence of rights reflected in *Rodriguez* indicates that, at least on the Constitutional level, the United States economic system is not organized to benefit the worst-off in society. At the legislative level, however, federal and state governments have adopted a number of institu-

tions designed to benefit those who are less well off, including welfare, Medicaid, and free public education at the primary and secondary levels.

Question: What do such programs suggest about human attitudes towards risk and preferences for rules for allocating wealth and income?

3. SOCIAL CONTRACT AND STATUS QUO: WHOSE CONSTITUTION?

A Theory of Justice attracted the widespread attention of both economists and political philosophers not only because of Rawls' claim that rational individuals drafting a social contract would choose the maximin principle for the distribution of economic goods but also because of his arguments concerning the circumstances under which that choice should be made. Rawls' theory depends on his assumptions concerning the "original position" from which rational individuals negotiate the terms of the social contract. In reading the following materials, consider how a change in the circumstances of the original position might change the likely terms to which rational individuals would consent.

J. RAWLS, A THEORY OF JUSTICE *

(1971).

* * * [T]he original position of equality corresponds to the state of nature in the traditional theory of the social contract. This original position is not, of course, thought of as an actual historical state of affairs, much less as a primitive condition of culture. It is understood as a purely hypothetical situation characterized so as to lead to a certain conception of justice. * * *

* * *

The idea of the original position is to set up a fair procedure so that any principles agreed to will be just. * * * Now in order to do this I assume that the parties are situated behind a veil of ignorance. They do not know how the various alternatives will affect their own particular case and they are obliged to evaluate principles solely on the basis of general considerations.

It is assumed, then, that the parties do not know certain kinds of particular facts. First of all, no one knows his place in society, his class position or social status; nor does he know his fortune in the distribution of natural assets and abilities, his intelligence and strength, and like. * * * More than this, I assume that the parties do not know the particular circumstances of their own society. That is, they do not

* Reprinted by permission of the publishers from A THEORY OF JUSTICE by John Rawls, Cambridge, Mass.: The Belknap Press of Harvard University Press, Copyright © 1971 by the President and Fellows of Harvard College.

know its economic or political situation, or the level of civilization and culture it has been able to achieve. * * *

* * *

The restrictions on particular information in the original position are * * * of fundamental importance. Without them we would not be able to work out any definite theory of justice at all. We would have to be content with a vague formula stating that justice is what would be agreed to without being able to say much, if anything, about the substance of the agreement itself. * * * The veil of ignorance makes possible a unanimous choice of a particular concept of justice. Without these limitations on knowledge the bargaining problem of the original position would be hopelessly complicated. Even if theoretically a solution were to exist, we would not, at present anyway, be able to determine it.

* * *

* * * [T]he reasons for the veil of ignorance go beyond mere simplicity. We want to define the original position so that we get the desired solution. If a knowledge of particulars is allowed, then the outcome is biased by arbitrary contingencies. As already observed, to each according to his threat advantage is not a principle of justice. If the original position is to yield agreements that are just, the parties must be fairly situated and treated equally as moral persons. The arbitrariness of the world must be corrected for by adjusting the circumstances of the initial contractual situation. * * *

Notes and Questions

1. Rawls gives two reasons why individuals in the original position should be denied information concerning their likely place in society as well as their likely abilities, talents, and advantages. The first reason is that ignorance is necessary in order to ensure that the terms of the social contract are just. Rawls believes that those who are strongest or most capable should not be allowed to exploit those advantages while negotiating the social contract. Recall Rawls' suggestion, above, that his two principles of justice "seem to be fair agreement on the basis of which those better endowed, or more fortunate in their social position, *neither of which we can be said to deserve,* could expect the willing cooperation of others" (emphasis added). The veil of ignorance ensures that persons in the original position bargain from a posture of equality as moral persons. "If no one knows his situation in society nor his natural assets * * * no one is in a position to tailor principles to his advantage." A Theory of Justice 139 (1971).

Question: Does the justice of the social contract negotiated behind a veil of ignorance depend on whether one agrees with Rawls' assertion that individuals do not deserve their social positions or natural endowments?

2. Rawls' second reason for arguing that the social contract should be drafted behind the veil of ignorance is that ignorance is a practical necessity to achieve unanimous agreement on the contract's terms.

Questions: How will bargaining among people who know their likely advantages and disadvantages differ from bargaining among people in a position of ignorant equality? In which case will unanimous agreement be harder to achieve?

DRED SCOTT v. SANDFORD

Supreme Court of the United States, 1856.
60 U.S. (19 How.) 393, 15 L.Ed. 691.

TANEY, CHIEF JUSTICE.

* * *

The plaintiff in error, who was also the plaintiff in the court below, was, with his wife and children, held as slaves by the defendant, in the State of Missouri; and he brought this action in the Circuit Court of the United States for that district, to assert the title of himself and his family to freedom.

The declaration * * * contains the averment necessary to give the court jurisdiction; that he and the defendant are citizens of different States; that is, that he is a citizen of Missouri, and the defendant a citizen of New York.

* * *

The question is simply this: Can a negro, whose ancestors were imported into this country, and sold as slaves, become a member of the political community formed and brought into existence by the Constitution of the United States, and as such become entitled to all the rights, and privileges, and immunities, guaranteed by that instrument to the citizen? One of which rights is the privilege of suing in a court of the United States in the cases specified in the Constitution.

* * *

The words "people of the United States" and "citizens" are synonymous terms, and mean the same thing. They both describe the political body who, according to our republican institutions, form the sovereignty, and who hold the power and conduct the Government through their representatives. They are what we familiarly call the "sovereign people," and every citizen is one of this people, and a constituent member of this sovereignty. The question before us is, whether the class of persons described in the plea in abatement compose a portion of this people, and are constituent members of this sovereignty? We think they are not, and that they are not included, and were not intended to be included, under the word "citizens" in the Constitution, and can therefore claim none of the rights and privileges which that instrument provides for and secures to citizens of the United States. On the contrary, they were at that time considered as a subordinate and inferior class of beings, who had been subjugated by the dominant race, and, whether emancipated or not, yet remained subject to their authority, and had no rights or privileges but such as those who held the power and the Government might choose to grant them.

It is not the province of the court to decide upon the justice or injustice, the policy or impolicy, of these laws. The decision of that question belonged to the political or law-making power; to those who formed the sovereignty and framed the Constitution. The duty of the court is, to interpret the instrument they have framed, with the best lights we can obtain on the subject, and to administer it as we find it, according to its true intent and meaning when it was adopted.

* * *

In the opinion of the court, the legislation and histories of the times, and the language used in the Declaration of Independence, show, that neither the class of persons who had been imported as slaves, nor their descendants, whether they had become free or not, were then acknowledged as a part of the people, nor intended to be included in the general words used in that memorable instrument.

* * *

The language of the Declaration of Independence is equally conclusive:

It begins by declaring that, "when in the course of human events it becomes necessary for one people to dissolve the political bands which have connected them with another, and to assume among the powers of the earth the separate and equal station to which the laws of nature and nature's God entitle them, a decent respect for the opinions of mankind requires that they should declare the causes which impel them to the separation."

It then proceeds to say: "We hold these truths to be self-evident: that all men are created equal; that they are endowed by their Creator with certain unalienable rights; that among them is life, liberty, and the pursuit of happiness; that to secure these rights, Governments are instituted, deriving their just powers from the consent of the governed."

The general words above quoted would seem to embrace the whole human family, and if they were used in a similar instrument at this day would be so understood. But it is too clear for dispute, that the enslaved African race were not intended to be included, and formed no part of the people who framed and adopted this declaration * * *.

* * *

* * * [T]here are two clauses in the Constitution which point directly and specifically to the negro race as a separate class of persons, and show clearly that they were not regarded as a portion of the people or citizens of the Government then formed.

One of these clauses reserves to each of the thirteen States the right to import slaves until the year 1808, if it thinks proper. * * * And by the other provision the States pledge themselves to each other to maintain the right of property of the master, by delivering up to him any slave who may have escaped from his service, and be found within their respective territories. * * * And these two provisions show, conclusively, that neither the description of persons therein referred to, nor their descendants, were embraced in any of the other provisions of the Constitution; for certainly these two clauses were not intended to confer on them or their posterity the blessings of liberty, or any of the personal rights so carefully provided for the citizen.

* * *

Upon the whole, therefore, it is the judgment of this court, that it appears by the record before us that the plaintiff in error is not a citizen of Missouri, in the sense in which that word is used in the Constitution; and that the Circuit Court of the United States, for that reason, had no jurisdiction in the case, and could give no judgment in it. Its judgment for the defendant must, consequently, be reversed, and a mandate issued, directing the suit to be dismissed for want of jurisdiction.

Notes and Questions

1. In Rawls' vision of the original position, individuals are stripped to their moral beings and negotiate the basic terms of society in ignorance of their future places in it. Such an arrangement necessarily leads to concern for those less well off in society, since each party to the agreement risks ending up in that position.

The Constitution of the United States was drafted by individuals aware of their own circumstances, which included: a large portion of the population lived in slavery and were regarded as property rather than citizens; women were presumed unfit to govern themselves or enjoy the full rights of citizenship, including the right to vote; and a small propertied class enjoyed a disproportionate amount of wealth, power, and privilege.

Question: How are those circumstances reflected in the Constitution?

2. In addition to arguing that individuals in the original position should have no knowledge of their likely place in the society they are forming, Rawls also argued (A Theory of Justice 137 (1971)):

> The persons in the original position [should] have no information as to which generation they belong. These broader restrictions on knowledge are appropriate in part because questions of social justice arise between generations as well as within them, for example, the questions of the appropriate rate of capital saving and of the conservation of natural resources and the environment of nature. * * * [I]n order to carry through the idea of the original position, the parties * * * must choose principles the consequences of which they are prepared to live with whatever generation they turn out to belong to.

Questions: Members of future generations could not participate in the U.S. Constitution's drafting. What provision does the Constitution make for future generations' interests? Must tomorrow's Americans rely upon the altruism and generosity of today's? Consider future Americans' interests in present policy on education, the federal deficit, and the environment. If future generations do not participate in negotiating the social contract, how is that likely to affect society's structure?

3. A compelling aspect of Rawls' theory is his normative claim that individuals should choose a social contract behind a veil of ignorance so that "no one is advantaged or disadvantaged in the choice of principles by the outcome of natural chance or the contingency of social circumstances" and all negotiate as equal "moral persons". A Theory of Justice 12 (1971). Individuals should not be allowed to exploit their natural advantages such as strength, energy, or intelligence. Those are acquired only through "chance;" they are not "deserved."

In Sierra Club v. Morton, 405 U.S. 727, 92 S.Ct. 1361, 31 L.Ed.2d 636 (1972), the Sierra Club challenged a U.S. Forest Service plan to allow Walt Disney Enterprises, Inc. to build a ski resort and summer recreation area in the Mineral King Valley adjacent to Sequoia National Park. Sierra Club alleged that the development "would destroy or otherwise adversely affect the scenery, natural and historic objects and wildlife of the park and would impair the enjoyment of the park for future generations." 405 U.S. at 734, 92 S.Ct. at 1365. The Supreme Court upheld the Ninth Circuit's determination that the Club lacked standing under the Administrative Procedure Act because none of the Club's individual members had alleged injury, and the Club could not sue as a general representative of the public interest.

In an impassioned dissent, Justice Douglas declared, 405 U.S. at 741–43, 752, 92 S.Ct. at 1369–70, 1374:

> The critical question of "standing" would be simplified and also put neatly in focus if we fashioned a federal rule that allowed environmental issues to be litigated before federal agencies or federal courts in the name of the inanimate object about to be despoiled, defaced, or invaded by roads and bulldozers * * *
>
> Inanimate objects are sometimes parties in litigation. A ship has a legal personality * * * The ordinary corporation is a "person" for purposes of the adjudicatory processes, whether it represents proprietary, spiritual, aesthetic, or charitable causes.
>
> So it should be as respects valleys, alpine meadows, rivers, lakes, estuaries, beaches, ridges, groves of trees, swampland, or even air that feels the destructive pressures of modern technology and modern life. * * *
>
> * * *
>
> * * * [E]nvironmental issues should be tendered by the inanimate object itself. Then there will be assurances that all of the forms of life which it represents will stand before the court—the pileated woodpecker as well as the coyote and bear, the lemmings as well as the trout in the streams. * * *

Questions: The Administrative Procedure Act, like many federal statutes, provides a cause of action for "a *person* suffering legal wrong." 5 U.S.C. § 702. As Justice Douglas pointed out, the American legal system recognizes as "persons" not only natural persons but also certain legal personalities such as corporations. The concept of person is not, however, normally extended to wildlife, vegetation, or natural wonders. From an economic perspective, does that make sense? Does it matter if society's goal is wealth maximization or utility maximization? Does Justice Douglas' dissent in *Sierra* imply that trout and coyotes are also moral persons behind the veil of ignorance?

4. Because Rawls' original position of ignorant equality is not a real state, it is a normative act to draft a social contract as if it were. How far one wants to proceed towards ignorant equality in constitutional bargaining is a question for the philosopher more than the economist. The economist takes preexisting distributions of advantages and disadvantages as given. She is concerned with allocating resources efficiently given the status quo, not with the justice of the status quo.

B. TRANSLATING INDIVIDUAL PREFERENCES INTO PUBLIC CHOICES: VOTING RULES AS INDICIA OF SOCIAL WELFARE

Identifying the goal of state coercion is only the first step in drafting a social contract. The next is deciding which resource allocations best accomplish that goal. Consider a beneficial but polluting technology like the internal combustion engine. How should a utilitarian state regulate such a technology? The aim is the greatest possible increase in utility (or, at least, the minimum decrease). The difficulty is determining which allocation of resources produces the most utility. How much disutility does society suffer from dirty air, and how much utility does it gain from the automobile? Individual preferences for clean air and mobility must somehow be translated into optimal social choices.

In markets, individuals express their preferences for goods and services through their willingness and ability to pay. In the political arena, individuals express their preferences for the goods produced by government—pollution regulation, police protection, public education—through voting. This section examines from an economic perspective the problems associated with using votes to translate individual preferences into social choices.

The discussion below divides voting rules into two broad categories. The first is unanimity voting, which requires that each member of a group consent to a proposed group action. The second category includes any rule that allows action based on less-than-unanimous agreement, such as plurality voting, traditional majority voting, and "supermajority" provisions requiring two-thirds or three-quarters approval. Under the rule of unanimity the group will only act if no one is left worse off as a result. Unanimity voting ensures that social choices pass Pareto's strict criteria. Unfortunately, reaching unanimous agreement can be difficult and time consuming and sometimes impossible. Allowing group action based on majority rule makes group decisionmaking easier and simpler and increases the range of actions that the group can approve. However, as discussed below, less-than-unanimity voting creates a risk of group action that actually decreases overall utility.

The cases presented below provide contexts for discussing the efficiency implications of group decisions under unanimity and less-than-unanimity voting. Those implications are important because the United States political system relies heavily on voting rules (and especially less-than-unanimity rules) for making public choices. For example, citizens vote to elect Representatives to Congress under a plurality system; Congress in turn votes on public legislation, generally under traditional majority rule. Rational maximizers drafting a social contract would want to consider the costs and risks of voting rules in deciding how group decisions should be made. The final section of this Chapter applies public choice analysis to the United States Constitution and considers how that document's provisions may minimize the costs of group action and the risk of erroneous social choices.

1. THE RULE OF UNANIMITY

A series of Supreme Court cases decided in the first half of the twentieth century appeared to assume that the Sixth Amendment right to a jury trial in federal criminal cases included a right to a unanimous jury verdict for conviction. See Andres v. United States, 333 U.S. 740, 748–49, 68 S.Ct. 880, 884–85, 92 L.Ed. 1055 (1948); Patton v. United States, 281 U.S. 276, 288–90, 50 S.Ct. 253, 254–55, 74 L.Ed. 854 (1930); Hawaii v. Mankichi, 190 U.S. 197, 211–12, 23 S.Ct. 787, 788, 47 L.Ed. 1016 (1903). That question was revisited in Apodaca v. Oregon and a related case, Johnson v. Louisiana, 406 U.S. 356, 92 S.Ct. 1620, 32 L.Ed.2d 152 (1972), where the Court addressed directly whether the Constitution required a unanimous verdict for criminal conviction and whether, if such a right existed under federal law, it should be incorporated under the Fourteenth Amendment and applied to criminal convictions in State courts as well.

APODACA v. OREGON

Supreme Court of the United States, 1972.
406 U.S. 404, 92 S.Ct. 1628, 32 L.Ed.2d 184.

WHITE, JUSTICE.

Robert Apodaca, Henry Morgan Cooper, Jr., and James Arnold Madden were convicted respectively of assault with a deadly weapon, burglary in a dwelling, and grand larceny before separate Oregon juries, all of which returned less-than-unanimous verdicts. The vote in the cases of Apodaca and Madden was 11–1, while the vote in the case of Cooper was 10–2, the minimum requisite vote under Oregon law for sustaining a conviction. After their convictions had been affirmed by the Oregon Court of Appeals, and review had been denied by the Supreme Court of Oregon, all three sought review in this Court upon a claim that conviction of crime by a less-than-unanimous jury violates the right to trial by jury in criminal cases specified by the Sixth Amendment and made applicable to the States by the Fourteenth. We granted certiorari to consider this claim, which we now find to be without merit.

* * *

Like the requirement that juries consist of 12 men, the requirement of unanimity arose during the Middle Ages and had become an accepted feature of the common-law jury by the 18th century. But * * * "the relevant constitutional history casts considerable doubt on the easy assumption * * * that if a given feature existed in a jury at common law in 1789, then it was necessarily preserved in the Constitution." * * *

* * *

Our inquiry must focus upon the function served by the jury in contemporary society. * * * [T]he purpose of trial by jury is to prevent oppression by the Government by providing a "safeguard against the corrupt or overzealous prosecutor and against the compliant, biased, or eccentric judge." * * * Requiring unanimity would obviously produce hung juries in some situations where nonunanimous juries will convict or acquit. But in either case, the interest of the defendant in having the judgment of his peers interposed between himself and the officers of the State who prosecute and judge him is equally well served.

* * *

Petitioners also cite quite accurately a long line of decisions of this Court upholding the principle that the Fourteenth Amendment requires jury panels to reflect a cross section of the community. They then contend that unanimity is a necessary precondition for effective application of the cross-section requirement, because a rule permitting less than unanimous verdicts will make it possible for convictions to occur without the acquiescence of minority elements within the community.

There are two flaws in this argument. One is petitioners' assumption that every distinct voice in the community has a right to be represented on every jury and a right to prevent conviction of a defendant in any case. * * * No group * * * has the right to block convictions; it has only the right to participate in the overall legal processes by which criminal guilt and innocence are determined.

We also cannot accept petitioners' second assumption—that minority groups, even when they are represented on a jury, will not adequately represent the viewpoint of those groups simply because they maybe outvoted in the final result. They will be present during all deliberations, and their views will be heard. We cannot assume that the majority of the jury will refuse to weigh the evidence and reach a decision upon rational grounds, just as it must now do in order to obtain unanimous verdicts, or that a majority will deprive a man of his liberty on the basis of prejudice when a minority is presenting a reasonable argument in favor of acquittal. * * *

* * *

Judgment affirmed.

POWELL, JUSTICE, concurring.

* * *

In an unbroken line of cases reaching back into the late 1800's, the Justices of this Court have recognized, virtually without dissent, that unanimity is one of the indispensable features of *federal* jury trial. * * * It therefore seems to me, in accord with both history and precedent, that the Sixth Amendment requires a unanimous jury verdict to convict in a federal criminal trial.

* * *

The question, therefore, that should be addressed in this case is whether unanimity is in fact so fundamental to the essentials of jury trial that this particular requirement of the Sixth Amendment is necessarily binding on the States under the Due Process Clause of the Fourteenth Amendment. An affirmative answer * * * would give unwarranted and unwise scope to the incorporation doctrine as it applies to the due process right of state criminal defendants to trial by jury.

* * *

* * * In an age in which empirical study is increasingly relied upon as a foundation for decisionmaking, one of the more obvious merits of our federal system is the opportunity it affords each State, if its people so choose, to become a "laboratory" and to experiment with a range of trial and procedural alternatives. * * * [This] might well lead to valuable innovations with respect to determining—fairly and more expeditiously—the guilt or innocence of the accused.

* * * I see no constitutional infirmity in the provision adopted by the people of Oregon. It * * * appears to be patterned on a provision of the American Law Institute's Code of Criminal Procedure. A similar decision has been echoed more recently in England where the unanimity requirement was abandoned by statutory enactment. Less-than-unanimous verdict provisions also have been viewed with approval by the American Bar Association's Criminal Justice Project. Those who have studied the jury mechanism and recommended deviation from the historic rule of unanimity have found a number of considerations to be significant. Removal of the unanimity requirement could well minimize the potential for hung juries occasioned either by bribery or juror irrationality. Furthermore, the rule that juries must speak with a single voice often leads, not to full agreement among the 12 but to agreement by none and compromise by all, despite the frequent absence of a rational basis for such compromise. Quite apart from whether Justices sitting on this Court would have deemed advisable the adop-

tion of any particular less-than-unanimous jury provision, I think that considerations of this kind reflect a legitimate basis for experimentation and deviation from the federal blueprint.

* * *

DOUGLAS, JUSTICE, dissenting.

* * *

The plurality approves a procedure which diminishes the reliability of a jury. First, it eliminates the circumstances in which a minority of jurors (a) could have rationally persuaded the entire jury to acquit, or (b) while unable to persuade the majority to acquit, nonetheless could have convinced them to convict only on a lesser-included offense. * * *

The diminution of verdict reliability flows from the fact that nonunanimous juries need not debate and deliberate as fully as must unanimous juries. As soon as the requisite majority is attained, further consideration is not required either by Oregon or by Louisiana even though the dissident jurors might, if given the chance, be able to convince the majority. * * * Indeed, if a necessary majority is immediately obtained, then no deliberation at all is required in these States. (There is a suggestion that this may have happened in the 10—2 verdict rendered in only 41 minutes in Apodaca's case.) To be sure, * * * initial majorities normally prevail in the end, but about a tenth of the time the rough-and-tumble of the jury room operates to reverse completely their preliminary perception of guilt or innocence. The Court now extracts from the jury room this automatic check against hasty factfinding by relieving jurors of the duty to hear out fully the dissenters.

It is said that there is no evidence that majority jurors will refuse to listen to dissenters whose votes are unneeded for conviction. Yet human experience teaches that polite and academic conversation is no substitute for the earnest and robust argument necessary to reach unanimity. As mentioned earlier, in Apodaca's case, whatever courtesy dialogue transpired could not have lasted more than 41 minutes. * * *

* * *

Moreover, even where an initial majority wins the dissent over to its side, the ultimate result in unanimous-jury States may nonetheless reflect the reservations of uncertain jurors. I refer to many compromise verdicts on lesser-included offenses and lesser sentences. Thus, even though a minority may not be forceful enough to carry the day, their doubts may nonetheless cause a majority to exercise caution. Obviously, however, in Oregon and Louisiana, dissident jurors will not have the opportunity through full deliberation to temper the opposing faction's degree of certainty of guilt.

The new rule also has an impact on cases in which a unanimous jury would have neither voted to acquit nor to convict, but would have deadlocked. In unanimous-jury States, this occurs about 5.6% of the time. * * *

* * *

Notes and Questions

1. In his concurrence in *Apodaca,* Justice Powell argued that, while the Sixth Amendment required a unanimous verdict in federal criminal cases, that requirement should not be imposed on states under the Fourteenth Amendment because it would discourage state experimentation with different means of determining the defendant's guilt or innocence "more expeditiously."

Question: What advantages of allowing 10–2 convictions rather than requiring unanimity does *Apodaca* suggest?

2. The requirement of unanimity was once typical of shareholder voting on "fundamental" corporate changes. Under nineteenth-century common law, a corporation could not dissolve, merge, amend its charter, or sell substantially all its assets unless each and every shareholder agreed to such action. The Supreme Court discussed the traditional rule of shareholder unanimity in Voeller v. Neilston Warehouse Co., 311 U.S. 531, 535 n. 6, 61 S.Ct. 376, 377 n. 6, 85 L.Ed. 322 (1941): "At common law, unanimous shareholder consent was a prerequisite to fundamental changes in the corporation. This made it possible for an arbitrary minority to establish a nuisance value for its shares by refusal to cooperate. To meet the situation, legislatures authorized the making of changes by majority vote."

Question: To appreciate what the Court meant by the "nuisance value" of refusing to cooperate, consider the following example. A corporation has ten shareholders, each of whom owns one share. Each share has a market value of $8. A third party offers to buy the firm for $20 per share. What strategic opportunities would a requirement of unanimity present to each of the shareholders?

3. In the nineteenth century, the typical corporation was a relatively small entity controlled by a single individual or group of individuals who ran the business together and dealt regularly with one another. In the twentieth century the typical corporation became larger, with a greater number of shareholders, some of whom might not be involved in the business at all. Under the typical modern state corporation statute, a corporation may dissolve, merge, or sell all its assets with the approval of from 50% to 75% of the firm's shareholders.

Questions: How does increasing the size of a decisionmaking body affect the time spent in decisionmaking? The likelihood of deadlock? The probability of strategic hold-out behavior? Can the increased size and complexity of twentieth century corporations explain why state legislatures abandoned shareholder unanimity in favor of less-than-unanimity rules? How are decisionmaking time, deadlock, and hold-out behavior changed by reducing the voting requirement from unanimity to 75% group approval? From 75% to 51% approval?

4. A footnote to Justice White's opinion in *Apodaca,* at 406 U.S. at 407–08 n.2, 92 S.Ct. at 1631–32 n.2 (1971), noted that while the origins of the common-law rule requiring jury unanimity rule were obscure, one possible explanation was:

> [J]ury unanimity arose out of the medieval concept of consent. Indeed, "(t)he word consent (*consensus*) carried with it the idea of concordia or unanimity * * * ." Even in 14th century Parliaments there is evidence that a majority vote was deemed insufficient to bind the community or individual members of the community to a legal decision; a unanimous decision was preferred. It was only in the 15th century that the decisionmaking process in Parliament became avowedly majoritarian, as the ideal of unanimity became increasingly difficult to attain.

Compare the medieval focus on unanimity with Justice Harlan's argument in Jacobson v. Massachusetts, 197 U.S. 11, 37–38, 25 S.Ct. 358, 366–69, 49 L.Ed. 643 (1905):

> We are not prepared to hold that a minority * * * may thus defy the will of its constituted authorities, acting in good faith for all, under the legislative sanction of the State. If such be the privilege of a minority then a like privilege would belong to each individual of the community, and the spectacle would be presented of the welfare and safety of an entire population being subordinated to the notions of a single individual who chooses to remain a part of that population.

> *Question:* From the perspective of utility maximization, how does the distinction between unanimity and less-than-unanimity voting rules resemble the distinction between the Pareto and the Kaldor–Hicks criteria?

5. Justice White's opinion for the majority in *Apodaca* suggested that allowing less-than-unanimous jury verdicts did not necessarily exclude the views of minority dissenters, as they might still voice their opinions during the jury deliberation process. Justice Brennan wrote a dissent in *Apodaca,* in which he argued, 406 U.S. at 596, 92 S.Ct. at 1651:

> When verdicts must be unanimous, no member of the jury may be ignored by the others. When less than unanimity is sufficient, consideration of minority views may become nothing more than a matter of majority grace. In my opinion, the right of all groups in this Nation to participate in the criminal process means the right to have their voices heard. A unanimous verdict vindicates that right. Majority verdicts could destroy it.

> *Question:* Whose arguments are more persuasive on the issue of minority participation in the decisionmaking process, Justice White's or Justice Brennan's?

6. Justices Powell and Douglas subscribed in their opinions to belief that divided juries often produce "compromise verdicts," convicting the defendant of a lesser-included offense or convicting the defendant but imposing a relatively light sentence. Justice Powell appeared to regard compromise verdicts as undesirable, while Justice Douglas regarded them as beneficial.

> *Questions:* What are the advantages and disadvantages of encouraging compromise? Is compromise more likely under a rule of unanimity or under a rule allowing less-than-unanimous verdicts?

7. Where jury unanimity is required, unanimous agreement is essential for *either* acquittal or conviction. Under the double jeopardy clause, if a jury fails to reach a unanimous verdict a prosecutor is free to treat the verdict as a nullity rather than as an acquittal and to seek a new trial. While a deadlock does not preclude a second trial, it does mean that the first trial was in a sense "wasted."

> *Questions:* Who is more likely to benefit from the requirement that criminal jury verdicts be unanimous, the prosecution or the accused? If hung juries squander the resources allocated to trial, why should Justice Douglas be concerned that allowing less-than-unanimous jury verdicts might produce *fewer* deadlocks?

2. SUPERMAJORITY, MAJORITY, AND PLURALITY VOTING RULES

Given the practical difficulties of requiring unanimity, especially when large numbers are involved, it should not be surprising that unanimity voting is the exception in most circumstances where groups are called upon to make decisions. The United States political system makes great use of less-than-unanimity voting rules, including plurality, traditional majority, and supermajority rules. Less-than-unanimity rules share common characteristics that distinguish them sharply from decisions reached unanimously. This section considers some of the economic implications of state action over a dissenting minority's protests.

a. Arrow's Theorem and Solutions to the Indeterminacy of Majority Rule

One political authority that frequently uses less-than-unanimous decisions as a basis for group action is the appellate court. When appellate judges disagree, the judgment normally is determined by what a majority of the panel sitting on the case believe the case's outcome should be. The court's opinion will be the opinion with the support of the largest number of judges concurring in the judgment.

The less-than-unanimity voting rules applied by appellate courts allow courts to reach more decisions more quickly than a rule of unanimity would. At the same time, appellate decisionmaking suggests some of the problems associated with majority rule.

F. EASTERBROOK, WAYS OF CRITICIZING THE COURT *

95 Harv.L.Rev. 802 (1982).

* * *

Everyone thinks that the Court should be consistent. Consistency is, it seems, an essential attribute of any institution that decides on the basis of statutes, constitutions, and criteria other than the Justices' preferences. The Court cannot logically say in December that a criminal defendant has a "valued right" to a jury verdict and in May that the deprivation of this right is irrelevant. Similarly, it cannot say that freedom of speech is a more important constitutional value than a defendant's right to a fair trial, that fair trial is more important than military preparedness, and that military preparedness is more important than free speech. To do so is to say that at least one decision is wrong or that they do not rest on the same document. Thus the propositions that decisions must be consistent, that principles must be followed unless the decisions announcing them are overruled, and that decisions rest on principles of general applicability are put by the Court's critics as logical implications of the proposition that the Court is supposed to follow statutes and a written Constitution. If this is so, an inconsistent Court is a willful, irresponsible Court.

Yet while admitting that it is bound by the written documents, the Court continues to hand down inconsistent decisions, to dishonor precedents, and to change the weight attached to particular constitutional and statutory provisions or the values derived from them. * * *

I * * * offer a different perspective. Inconsistency is inevitable, in the strong sense of that word, no matter how much the Justices may disregard their own preferences, no matter how carefully they may approach their tasks, no matter how skilled they may be. * * * [D]emands for perfect consistency can not be fulfilled, and it is inappropriate to condemn the Court's performance as an institution simply by pointing out that it sometimes, even frequently, contradicts itself.

The argument in the following pages is based on the developing theory of public choice. The theory is an outgrowth of the work of Kenneth Arrow, whose book *Social Choice and Individual Values,* published in 1951, prompted an explosion of work by economists and political scientists that has become a separate discipline. Arrow's followers began to examine with great care the operation of all systems for making collective choices: that is, methods of pooling individual preferences and decisions to arrive at a decision for the group. This work almost always concerns voting mechanisms * * *.

* * *

The Court decides cases by majority vote. Its ability to make consistent, principled decisions therefore depends on the existence of a system of voting that produces such outcomes. Yet voting systems are subject to many problems. First, decisions produced by voting will tend to be unstable even when the same voters participate in all decisions; second, the sequence in which issues are decided frequently controls the outcome of the process * * *.

* * *

Suppose the Justices have studied the establishment clause, and different Justices reach different conclusions about the meaning of that provision. * * * Three Justices conclude that all public acts that directly or indirectly aid religion violate the clause; call this Position A for absolutism. Three more conclude that any public act is constitutional if it is neutral between religious and nonreligious associations (N for neutrality). The remaining three conclude that the clause requires balancing, in which the purpose of the act, its effect on religion, and the extent of entanglement between state and religion all play a role (B for balancing). It is a detail that three Justices have each position; the problem would be the same (although the presentation would be more complicated) if the numbers were different and there were more than three interpretations of the clause.

Each group of Justices, moreover, has a preference between the two positions taken by the others. The Justices who take position N (neutrality) [group 1] may believe that position B (balancing) more accurately reflects the design of the framers an the Court's cases than does position A (absolute ban on aid). The Justices who take position B [group 2] may conclude that A is more nearly correct than N. And the Justices who take position A [group 3] may conclude that N is more nearly correct than B. This last is not as odd as it first appears: these Justices conclude that the clause embodies a bright line test and that any attempt at balancing is worse than either bright line test because it immerses the Court in the details of a process properly left to the legislature.

* * * When a case under the establishment clause comes before the Court, the Justices always vote according to their conclusions. But this voting will not lead them to agree on a rule, no matter how they go about the task. They cannot settle on rule A, because the Justices in groups 2 and 3 (a majority) believe that rule B is a more accurate construction of the clause than rule A. Yet rule B cannot be chosen either, because a majority (those in groups 1 and 3) would select rule N over rule B. And, to complete the cycle, a majority (in groups 1 and 2) would select rule A over rule N. No matter what the Court does, a majority would always vote to change the rule.

* * *

* * * One of the most interesting findings of the public choice literature is that the decisions of any group are sensitive to the order in which it considers the options. One theorem states that it is possible to construct a decision path that ends with *any* rule, as long as each step is taken by majority vote and, at every step, earlier decisions are respected. * * *

* * *

The conclusion of this analysis is unsettling, as any application of Arrow's Theorem is unsettling. * * * Any general criticism of the Court, as an institution, for rendering inconsistent decisions is untenable. At least some inconsistency, and probably a great deal of inconsistency, is inevitable.

* * *

Notes and Questions

1. One of the most important developments in public choice theory was Kenneth Arrow's 1951 publication of his General Possibility Theorem, which is now widely known, because of his conclusions, as "Arrow's Impossibility Theorem." Arrow demonstrated that under certain conditions, groups attempting to choose among three or more alternatives by majority voting may be unable to reach a consistent decision.

Consider the following example. Larry, Curly, and Mo have to decide what they are going to do together Sunday afternoon. The friends have three options; tour an art gallery, go to the baseball game, or attend a matinee symphony concert. Larry prefers art to baseball and baseball to concerts; Curly prefers baseball to concerts and concerts to art; and Mo prefers concerts to art and art to baseball. In other words, the three friends' preference rankings are as follows:

Larry: art > baseball > concert
Curly: baseball > concert > art
Mo: concert > art > baseball

If Larry, Curly, and Mo attempt to choose an alternative by voting between art, baseball, and a concert in a series of pairwise votes, they will be unable to reach a stable decision. When they vote between a trip to the art gallery and baseball, a majority (Larry and Mo) will prefer the art gallery. When they vote between baseball and a concert, a majority (Larry and Curly) will prefer baseball. And when they vote between a concert and art, a majority (Curly and Mo) will prefer a concert. But how can this be, if baseball is preferred to a concert, and art preferred to baseball? The results of majority voting in this case are an unstable "cycle" in which the group first chooses the art gallery, then the baseball game, then the concert, then art again, and so on *ad infinitum.*

Questions: What does cycling suggest about the accuracy of majority voting as a method of deciding which option maximizes group welfare? Does unanimity voting share this characteristic of majority voting?

2. Arrow's proof examined whether a voting system could aggregate individual orderings (rankings) of preferences into a social ordering exhibiting the five following desirable characteristics:

(1) *Unanimity* (the Pareto postulate): If an individual's preferences are unopposed by any other group member, that individual's preferences will be respected in the social ordering. That is, the social ordering will prefer any change that makes at least one person better off while making no one worse off.

(2) *Nondictatorship:* No individual's preference may be the preference of the social ordering if it is opposed by all other individuals. That means no single individual may dictate society's choice, no matter how strongly that individual may feel about the matter.

(3) *Range* (unrestricted domain): Individuals may rank alternatives in any order they choose; in other words, individuals may prefer

any one of the many possible orderings of art, baseball, and a concert. There are no restrictions on the kinds of orderings that are possible.

(4) *Independence of Irrelevant Alternatives:* Individuals' choices between two alternatives are based solely on their relative preferences for those alternatives and not on their opinions of other "irrelevant" alternatives not being voted on at the time. This condition is designed in part to ensure that individuals do not strategically misrepresent their choices in order to influence voting in subsequent elections.

(5) *Transitivity:* The social ordering produced by voting is a stable and consistent ordering of all alternatives. If art is preferred to baseball and baseball is preferred to concerts, then concerts cannot be preferred to art. When the social ordering is intransitive (as in the example presented in the preceding question), voting systems produce unstable results or "cycling."

Arrow demonstrated that it was impossible to produce a social preference ranking based on individual rankings meeting all five of the above characteristics, hence the modern label "Impossibility Theorem." For a relatively simple exposition of the proof, see K. Arrow, Social Choice and Individual Values (2d ed.1963) 96–100; D. Mueller, Public Choice II 385–87 (1989).

3. On July 1, 1981, the Supreme Court handed down two Fourth Amendment search and seizure cases: New York v. Belton, 453 U.S. 454, 101 S.Ct. 2860, 69 L.Ed.2d 768 (1981) and Robbins v. California, 453 U.S. 420, 101 S.Ct. 2841, 69 L.Ed.2d 744 (1981). In *Belton,* a New York State trooper stopped a car for speeding, found marijuana on the floor of the vehicle, arrested the occupants, and then found cocaine when he unzipped and searched the pockets of a jacket one of the passengers had left on the car's back seat. Justices Stewart, Burger, Powell, Blackmun, Rehnquist, and Stevens believed the search was constitutional, while Justices Brennan, Marshall, and White dissented.

In *Robbins,* California Highway Patrol officers stopped the petitioner's stationwagon because he was driving erratically and then found marijuana inside the passenger compartment of the car. The officers searched the car further by opening the tailgate and lifting up the door to a recessed luggage compartment that contained two packages wrapped in opaque plastic. The officers unwrapped the packages and found 15 pounds of marijuana. Justices Stewart, Burger, Powell, Brennan, Marshall, and White believed the search and seizure should be struck down as a Fourth Amendment violation, while Justices Blackmun, Rehnquist, and Stevens dissented that the search was constitutional.

Justice Steven's dissent in *Robbins* declared that "[i]t is quite clear to most of us that this case and *New York v. Belton* should be decided in the same way. Both cases involve automobile searches. In both cases, the automobiles had been lawfully stopped on the highway, the occupants had been lawfully arrested, and the officers had probable cause to believe that the vehicles contained contraband." 453 U.S. at 444, 101 S.Ct. at 2855. Justice Stevens went on to observe in a footnote that "Justice Blackmun, Justice Rehnquist, and I would uphold the searches in both cases; Justice Brennan, Justice White, and Justice Marshall would invalidate both searches. Only The Chief Justice [Burger], Justice Stewart, and Justice Powell reach the curious conclusion that a citizen has a greater privacy interest in a package of marihuana enclosed in a plastic wrapper than in the pocket of a leather jacket." 453 U.S. at 444 n.1, 101 S.Ct. at 2855 n.1.

Suppose that the justices' preferences were as follows. Justices Blackmun, Rehnquist, and Stevens preferred upholding both searches to striking down both but preferred striking down both searches to upholding one and striking down the other. Justices Brennan, White, and Marshall preferred striking down both searches to upholding one and striking down the other and preferred upholding one and striking down the other to upholding both searches. And Chief Justice Burger and Justices Stewart and Powell preferred upholding one and striking down the other to upholding both searches but preferred upholding both to striking down both.

Question: How might the opinions in *Robbins* and *Belton* illustrate Arrow's Theorem?

4. Although Arrow proved cycling is *possible* under majority voting when the conditions of unanimity, range, nondictatorship, and independence of irrelevant alternatives apply, cycling is not the *inevitable* result of majority voting. Returning to the facts presented in Question 1, suppose that Larry, Curly and Mo ranked their options as follows:

Larry: art > baseball > concert
Curly: baseball > concert > art
Mo: concert > baseball > art

In such a case, baseball consistently wins in pairwise voting against either the art gallery or the symphony concert. An extreme example of the same point is three individuals who favor the same option—the art gallery, for instance—so that art wins consistently under majority voting. The more homogeneous voter preferences are, the more likely majority voting will produce stable results.

Questions: On what sorts of issues are voter preferences likely to be homogeneous? On what issues might preferences be very diverse, so that majority voting leads to unstable cycling? What effect has the number of available alternatives on voter homogeneity of preference?

Judge Easterbrook suggests that majority voting leads appellate courts to dishonor precedent and hand down inconsistent and unstable decisions. Yet another political authority that relies on majority voting—the representative legislature—appears to produce reasonably consistent and stable decisions. Legislatures rarely vote for a 65 m.p.h. speed limit this year, no speed limit at all the next, a 55 m.p.h. limit the third year, and a return to 65 m.p.h. the fourth. New laws tend to be passed in response to changing social conditions (for example, a gasoline shortage) rather than an inexplicable change of legislative heart.

It is puzzling that legislation exhibits such stability, especially when one considers that while judges are supposed to defer to precedent, legislators are free not to. Legislative stability hints at the limits of Arrow's Theorem. The three following cases provide contexts for discussing legislative solutions to cycling under majority rule. In reading them, consider whether the factors that lead to stable voting results also improve the *accuracy* of majority voting as a measure of social preferences.

KRAMER v. UNION FREE SCHOOL DISTRICT NO. 15

Supreme Court of the United States, 1969.
395 U.S. 621, 89 S.Ct. 1886, 23 L.Ed.2d 583.

WARREN, CHIEF JUSTICE.

In this case we are called on to determine whether § 2012 of the New York Education Law is constitutional. The legislation provides that in certain New York school districts residents who are otherwise eligible to vote in state and federal elections may vote in the school district election only if they (1) own (or lease) taxable real property within the district, or (2) are parents (or have custody of) children enrolled in the local public schools. Appellant, a bachelor who neither owns nor leases taxable real property, filed suit in federal court claiming that § 2012 denied him equal protection of the laws in violation of the Fourteenth Amendment. With one judge dissenting, a three-judge District Court dismissed appellant's complaint. Finding that § 2012 does violate the Equal Protection Clause of the Fourteenth Amendment, we reverse.

* * *

* * * Appellant agrees that the States have the power to impose reasonable citizenship, age, and residency requirements on the availability of the ballot. The sole issue in this case is whether the *additional* requirements of § 2012—requirements which prohibit some district residents who are otherwise qualified by age and citizenship from participating in district meetings and school board elections—violate the Fourteenth Amendment's command that no State shall deny persons equal protection of the laws.

* * * "(S)ince the right to exercise the franchise in a free and unimpaired manner is preservative of other basic civil and political rights, any alleged infringement of the right of citizens to vote must be carefully and meticulously scrutinized." This careful examination is necessary because statutes distributing the franchise constitute the foundation of our representative society. Any unjustified discrimination in determining who may participate in political affairs or in the selection of public officials undermines the legitimacy of representative government.

* * *

* * * Accordingly, when we are reviewing statutes which deny some residents the right to vote, the general presumption of constitutionality afforded state statutes and the traditional approval given state classifications if the Court can conceive of a "rational basis" for the distinctions made are not applicable. The presumption of constitutionality and the approval given "rational" classifications in other types of enactments are based on an assumption that the institutions of state government are structured so as to represent fairly all the people. However, when the challenge to the statute is in effect a challenge of this basic assumption, the assumption can no longer serve as the basis for presuming constitutionality. * * *

* * *

Appellant asserts that excluding him from participation in the district elections denies him equal protection of the laws. He contends that he and others of his class are substantially interested in and significantly affected by the school meeting decisions. All members of the community have an interest in the quality and structure of public education, appellant says, and he urges that "the decisions taken by local boards ... may have grave consequences to the entire population." Appellant also argues that the level of property taxation affects him, even though he does not own property, as property tax levels affect the price of goods and services in the community.

We turn therefore to question whether the exclusion is necessary to promote a compelling state interest. First, appellees argue that the State has a legitimate interest in limiting the franchise in school district elections to "members of the community of interest"—those "primarily interested in such elections." Second, appellees urge that the State may reasonably and permissibly conclude that "property taxpayers" (including lessees of taxable property who share the tax burden through rent payments) and parents of the children enrolled in the district's schools are those "primarily interested" in school affairs.

* * *

We need express no opinion as to whether the State in some circumstances might limit the exercise of the franchise to those "primarily interested" or "primarily affected." * * * For, assuming, *arguendo,* that New York legitimately might limit the franchise in these school district elections to those "primarily interested in school affairs," close scrutiny of the § 2012 classifications demonstrates that they do not accomplish this purpose with sufficient precision to justify denying appellant the franchise.

Whether classifications allegedly limiting the franchise to those resident citizens "primarily interested" deny those excluded equal protection of the laws depends, *inter alia,* on whether all those excluded are in fact substantially less interested or affected than those the statute includes. In other words, the classifications must be tailored so that the exclusion of appellant and members of his class is necessary to achieve the articulated state goal. Section 2012 does not meet the exacting standard of precision we require of statutes which selectively distribute the franchise. The classifications in § 2012 permit inclusion of many persons who have, at best, a remote and indirect interest, in school affairs and, on the other hand, exclude others who have a distinct and direct interest in the school meeting decisions.

* * * The requirements of § 2012 are not sufficiently tailored to limiting the franchise to those "primarily interested" in school affairs to justify the denial of the franchise to appellant and members of his class.

The judgment of the United States District Court for the Eastern District of New York is therefore reversed. The case is remanded for further proceedings consistent with this opinion.

It is so ordered.

STEWART, JUSTICE, dissenting.

* * *

* * * So long as the classification is rationally related to a permissible legislative end, therefore—as are residence, literacy, and age requirements imposed with respect to voting—there is no denial of equal protection.

Thus judged, the statutory classification involved here seems to me clearly to be valid. New York has made the judgment that local educational policy is best left to those persons who have certain direct and definable interests in that policy: those who are either immediately involved as parents of schoolchildren or who, as owners or lessees of taxable property are burdened with the local cost of funding school district operations. True, persons outside those classes may be genuinely interested in the conduct of a school district's business—just as commuters from New Jersey may be genuinely interested in the outcome of a New York City election. But unless this Court is to claim a monopoly of wisdom regarding the sound operation of school systems in the 50 States, I see no way to justify the conclusion that the legislative classification involved here is not rationally related to a legitimate legislative purpose. "There is no group more interested in the operation and management of the public schools than the taxpayers who support them and the parents whose children attend them."

With good reason, the Court does not really argue the contrary. Instead, it strikes down New York's statute by asserting that the traditional equal protection standard is inapt in this case, and that a considerably stricter standard—under which classifications relating to "the franchise" are to be subjected to "exacting judicial scrutiny"—should be applied. But the asserted justification for applying such a standard cannot withstand analysis.

* * *

* * * I am at a loss to understand how such reasoning is at all relevant to the present case. The voting qualifications at issue have

been promulgated, not by Union Free School District No. 15, but by the New York State Legislature, and the appellant is of course fully able to participate in the election of representatives in that body. There is simply no claim whatever here that the state government is not "structured so as to represent fairly all the people," including the appellant.

* * *

* * * I respectfully dissent from the Court's judgment and opinion.

Notes and Questions

1. Courts normally uphold state classifications of persons against challenges under the Equal Protection Clause if the classification is rationally related to a legitimate government objective. When a classification burdens an individual's fundamental rights, however, the court applies the more exacting standard of strict scrutiny and will strike down the classification scheme unless it is necessary to promote a compelling state objective. *Kramer* held that voting was a fundamental right under the Equal Protection clause and that § 2012's classification did not stand up to the strict scrutiny test.

Questions: According to the defendants in *Kramer,* the state objective promoted by § 2012 was restricting voting in rural school board elections to those community members most interested in the elections' outcomes. What sort of interests did plaintiff Kramer—a 31–year–old, childless, bachelor stockbroker living rent-free in his parents' home—claim in his district's school board elections? How do Kramer's interests compare with the interests of a homeowner with three school-age children?

2. Justice Stewart's dissent in *Kramer* observed that the plaintiff was fully able to participate in the election of members to the New York State Legislature, which passed § 2012's voting restriction.

Questions: Why might the New York State Legislature have wanted to restrict voting in school board elections? Could restricting voting on particular issues to those most directly affected improve the accuracy of voting outcomes so that voting decisions are more likely to maximize utility?

3. The appellants in *Kramer* did not dispute that states have the power to impose reasonable citizenship, age, and residency requirements for voting.

Question: How might such traditional voting restrictions serve the economic goal of maximizing utility?

4. Although the majority opinion in *Kramer* avoided the question of whether restricting elections to interested voters was a "legitimate" state objective, in subsequent cases the Court has upheld voter restrictions in elections to a limited-purpose governmental units.

Salyer Land Co. v. Tulare Lake Basin Water Storage District, 410 U.S. 719, 93 S.Ct. 1224, 35 L.Ed.2d 659 (1973), upheld a state voting restriction providing that only landowners within the Tulare Lake Basin Water

Storage District could elect officers to the District. The statute also determined the number of the landowner's votes according to the assessed value of his land. The Court emphasized that the water district had an extremely limited purpose and also that the district's decisions disproportionately affected the landowners who received nearly all the water benefits of the project but also bore all the costs, which were assessed against each landowner according to the benefits received.

Ball v. James, 451 U.S. 355, 101 S.Ct. 1811, 68 L.Ed.2d 150 (1981), upheld a similar provision restricting voting in elections to the Salt River Project Agricultural Improvement and Power District to landowners and apportioning votes according to the number of acres owned. However, unlike the Tulare Lake Basin District, the Salt River District raised the money for its water operations not by landowner assessments but primarily by selling electricity to hundreds of thousands of persons living in the metropolitan Phoenix area. The opinion in *Ball* emphasized the district's narrow purpose but appeared far less concerned about the impact of the district's policy decisions on non-voters, electricity consumers in particular. The Court upheld the restriction on the ground that it was a rational means for the state to pursue its objectives.

Question: From an economic perspective, which is more relevant to the accuracy of voting as a measure of group preferences, the limited purpose of a special government unit or the fact that the unit's impact is restricted to a particular group primarily affected by its policies?

5. Traditional voting is a binary process; the voter can express whether he is for or against a proposal, but cannot express *how much* he supports or opposes it. "Yea" may mean either enthusiastic endorsement or mild preference; "nay" may mean passionate opposition or slight disapproval.

Traditional voting's failure to reflect individuals' intensity of feeling makes voting a potentially inaccurate measure of group preferences and leads to the cycling possibilities implied by Arrow's Theorem. Attaching equal weight to the votes of the individual who slightly favors a proposal and the individual who vehemently opposes it presents an unavoidable risk of inefficient decisions. Consider how society's overall utility is reduced when a 51% majority approves an action which benefits each of them slightly but imposes great costs on each person in the 49% minority.

To measure the sum of individual preferences accurately, individuals must be able to express the degree of utility or disutility they associate with proposed actions. Suppose Larry, Curly and Mo could express the exact amount of utility (measured in utils [u.]) they derive from art, baseball, and concerts in the following fashion:

Larry: art (14 u.) > baseball (2 u.) > concert (1 u.)
Curly: baseball (8 u.) > concert (4 u.) > art (1 u.)
Mo: concert (3 u.) > baseball (2 u.) > art (1 u.)

Questions: Given cardinal information about individual preferences, can one determine which activity maximizes the total utility of the small society composed of Larry, Curly, and Mo? If the votes of each person were weighed by the amount of utility to be obtained by each outcome, would the results of pairwise voting be transitive or intransitive? Which activity would be selected under traditional binary pairwise majority voting?

6. Some voting methods attempt to take account of the intensity of voters' preferences. Consider cumulative or "point" voting schemes. Each voter is given a supply of votes and permitted to use them as she chooses. The voter may decide to cast a small number of ballots for a number of different proposals or candidates. Alternatively, the voter may pass on issues about which, or candidates about whom, she has no strong feelings and save her votes in order to cast them all at once for the single proposal or candidate she favors most strongly.

Corporate charters often provide for cumulative voting in directors' elections. For California corporations, this requirement is statutory. Section 708 of the California Corporations Code provides:

> [E]very shareholder * * * entitled to vote at any election of directors may cumulate such shareholder's votes and give one candidate a number of votes equal to the number of directors to be elected multiplied by the number of votes to which the shareholder's shares are normally entitled, or distribute the shareholder's votes on the same principle among as many candidates as the shareholder thinks fit * * *.

Suppose a California corporation has four shareholders. Each owns one share and is entitled to one vote. At the annual shareholders' meeting, an election is held to fill the four positions on the board of directors. One shareholder, John, desperately wants to elect Mary to the board. The other three shareholders—who hold a majority of shares and votes—agree to conspire against John and try to elect a slate of four other candidates to the Board.

> *Questions:* What would be the result of an election under traditional majority rule? How does cumulative voting incorporate John's intense preference for Mary as a director?

7. Voting in legislative bodies such as the U.S. Congress generally takes the form of traditional majority voting rather than point or cumulative voting. Nevertheless, individual legislators can express the intensity of their feelings on proposed legislation to some degree when the legislature is faced with a series of votes on differing issues. In such a case, a representative can concentrate her voting power not by saving and pooling her own votes (an impossibility under traditional majority rule) but by pooling her votes with other representatives'. The intensely concerned representative can persuade other representatives to vote with her on the bills about which she feels most strongly if she agrees to vote with them on the bills about which they feel most strongly.

The practice of trading votes—also known as *logrolling*—allows a legislator to accumulate voting strength on an issue about which she cares deeply. By voting in favor of proposals she mildly dislikes, she buys allies to support the proposal she strongly favors. Exchanging votes thus provides an indirect means of reflecting the intensity of preferences.

Questions: Can logrolling improve the accuracy of majority voting in legislative bodies? Can logrolling improve the accuracy of general elections in which voters select representatives to the legislature?

8. A third method for voters to express their intensity of preference—the simple buying and selling of votes—is expressly forbidden by law. If votes were sold on the market, voting power on a particular issue would end up in the hands of the person who valued it most highly as measured by willingness to pay.

Questions: From an economic perspective, what are the advantages of allowing a market in votes? What are the distributional implications of the inalienability of voting rights and the "one-person-one-vote" norm?

GREGG v. GEORGIA

Supreme Court of the United States, 1976.
428 U.S. 153, 96 S.Ct. 2909, 49 L.Ed.2d 859.

STEWART, JUSTICE.

* * *

The petitioner, Troy Gregg, was charged with committing armed robbery and murder. In accordance with Georgia procedure in capital cases, the trial was in two stages, a guilt stage and a sentencing stage. The evidence at the guilt trial established that on November 21, 1973, the petitioner and a traveling companion, Floyd Allen, while hitchhiking north in Florida were picked up by Fred Simmons and Bob Moore. * * * A short time later the four men interrupted their journey for a rest stop along the highway. The next morning the bodies of Simmons and Moore were discovered in a ditch nearby.

* * *

* * * The jury found the petitioner guilty of two counts of armed robbery and two counts of murder.

At the penalty stage, which took place before the same jury, neither the prosecutor nor the petitioner's lawyer offered any additional evidence. Both counsel, however, made lengthy arguments dealing generally with the propriety of capital punishment under the circumstances and with the weight of the evidence of guilt. The trial judge instructed the jury that it could recommend either a death sentence or a life prison sentence on each count. The judge further charged the jury that in determining what sentence was appropriate the jury was free to consider the facts and circumstances, if any, presented by the parties in mitigation or aggravation.

* * *

* * * [T]he jury returned verdicts of death on each count.

* * *

We address initially the basic contention that the punishment of death for the crime of murder is, under all circumstances, "cruel and unusual" in violation of the Eighth and Fourteenth Amendments of the Constitution. * * *

* * * [U]ntil *Furman v. Georgia,* the Court never confronted squarely the fundamental claim that the punishment of death always, regardless of the enormity of the offense or the procedure followed in imposing the sentence, is cruel and unusual punishment in violation of the Constitution. Although this issue was presented and addressed in *Furman,* it was not resolved by the Court. Four Justices would have held that capital punishment is not unconstitutional *per se;* two Justices would have reached the opposite conclusion; and three Justices, while agreeing that the statutes then before the Court were invalid as applied, left open the question whether such punishment may ever be imposed. We now hold that the punishment of death does not invariably violate the Constitution.

* * *

We now consider whether Georgia may impose the death penalty on the petitioner in this case.

While *Furman* did not hold that the infliction of the death penalty *per se* violates the Constitution's ban on cruel and unusual punishments, it did recognize that the penalty of death is different in kind from any other punishment imposed under our system of criminal justice. Because of the uniqueness of the death penalty, *Furman* held that it could not be imposed under sentencing procedures that created a substantial risk that it would be inflicted in an arbitrary and capricious manner. * * * [T]he death sentences examined by the Court in *Furman* were "cruel and unusual in the same way that being struck by lightening is cruel and unusual. * * * [T]he Eighth and Fourteenth Amendments cannot tolerate the infliction of a sentence of death under legal systems that permit this unique penalty to be so wantonly and freakishly imposed."

Furman mandates that where discretion is afforded a sentencing body on a matter so grave as the determination of whether a human life should be taken or spared, that discretion must be suitably directed and limited so as to minimize the risk of wholly arbitrary and capricious action.

* * *

Jury sentencing has been considered desirable in capital cases in order "to maintain a link between contemporary community values and the penal system * * * ." But it creates special problems. Much of the information that is relevant to the sentencing decision may have no relevance to the question of guilt, or may even be extremely prejudicial to a fair determination of that question. This problem, however, is scarcely insurmountable. Those who have studied the question suggest that a bifurcated procedure—one in which the question of sentence is not considered until the determination of guilt has been made—is the best answer.

* * *

For the reasons expressed in this opinion, we hold that the statutory system under which Gregg was sentenced to death does not violate the Constitution. Accordingly, the judgment of the Georgia Supreme Court is affirmed.

It is so ordered.

Notes and Questions

1. In upholding Georgia's death penalty statute, the majority in *Gregg* gave great weight to the fact that, under the bifurcated sentencing procedure, the jury first determined guilt or innocence and then, in a second proceeding, decided whether to impose the death penalty. The Court held that the bifurcated procedure, combined with other statutory provisions guiding the jurors' discretion, eliminated any substantial risk that the penalty would be inflicted in an "arbitrary and capricious" or "freakish" manner.

Consider the implications of Arrow's Theorem for whether a bifurcated trial would help ensure that the death penalty is not imposed capriciously in a hypothetical case where majority rule decides the outcome. Suppose a defendant is being tried by a jury of twelve in a case where the death penalty is an option and where the defendant can be convicted and sentenced on the basis of a two-thirds vote. There are three possible outcomes. The defendant may be acquitted; may be sentenced to life imprisonment; or may receive the death penalty.

Four of the jurors (Group 1) believe that the defendant probably did not commit the crime. If the defendant *did* commit the crime, however, they believe the death penalty should be imposed. Another four (Group 2) believe the defendant is guilty and should be imprisoned but loathe the notion of capital punishment and would rather let a guilty man go free than inflict it. The remaining four jurors believe the defendant is guilty and also believe capital punishment should be imposed. The preferences of the three groups can be described as follows:

Group 1: acquittal > death > imprisonment
Group 2: imprisonment > acquittal > death
Group 3: death > imprisonment > acquittal

The jury determines guilt and sentencing in a bifurcated proceeding like the one approved in *Gregg.* First, the jury votes on whether the defendant is innocent, or should be at least be imprisoned (acquittal versus imprisonment). A majority favor imprisonment. The jury next considers whether the death penalty should be imposed (imprisonment versus death). A majority prefer the death penalty to imprisonment, and the defendant is sentenced to death.

Questions: What would happen if the order of proceedings were reversed? In other words, suppose the jury chooses *first* between the death penalty and life imprisonment should the defendant be convicted (imprisonment versus death), and *then* decides guilt or innocence (death versus acquittal)?

2. The previous question suggests that the order of bifurcated proceedings in death penalty cases can affect the outcome of cases decided under majority rule. As a practical matter, states that allow the jury to recommend or demand the death penalty generally also require the jury's decision on that issue to be unanimous. But see Proffitt v. Florida, 428 U.S. 242, 96 S.Ct. 2960, 49 L.Ed.2d 913 (1976) (upholding Florida death penalty statute where judge sentences defendant after hearing jury's advisory verdict based on majority vote).

Question: Does bifurcation affect the outcome of voting under a rule of unanimity?

3. Arrow predicted that under certain conditions, majority voting leads to unstable cycling of results. However, cycling cannot occur when the individuals voting respect earlier decisions. For example, having decided that the defendant is guilty and should not be acquitted, and having chosen the death penalty over imprisonment, the jury refuses to revisit the issue of their preferences for acquittal versus the death penalty.

Question: Deciding to call a halt to voting and not revisit old issues is one way of overcoming cycling. Does respecting earlier decisions make voting a more accurate measure of social preferences or simply a more stable measure?

4. Judge Easterbrook noted in Ways of Criticizing the Court, above, that "[o]ne of the most interesting findings of the public choice literature is that the decisions of any group are sensitive to the order in which it considers the options." That characteristic of majority voting under Arrow's Theorem is sometimes described as "path dependence." If the group respects past decisions, the outcome of majority voting can depend on the path of group decisionmaking. Whether the defendant is executed or set free depends on whether guilt or penalty is decided first.

When the results of voting are path dependent, an individual can control the outcome of voting if he or she can control the agenda, the path of decisionmaking, by deciding the order in which issues are considered. By determining where the group begins, and where it calls a halt to voting, the agenda controller can break the cycling pattern at the most advantageous point.

The power to determine outcome by setting the agenda exists even when a series of pairwise votes would produce a consistently favored outcome instead of cycling. Suppose Larry, Curly, and Mo have the following preferences:

Larry: art > baseball > concert
Curly: baseball > art > concert
Mo: concert > baseball > art

In a series of pairwise votes, baseball will always defeat both the art gallery and the symphony concert. An option which triumphs over all other options in pairwise voting is called a *Condorcet winner,* after the Marquis de Condorcet, an eighteenth-century nobleman who may have been the first public choice theorist to discover the cycling implications of majority voting.

Suppose, however, that Larry, a public choice theorist, controls the agenda. He can ensure that the group picks his favorite option (the art gallery) by setting the following agenda. First, the three friends will vote baseball "up or down." In effect, the choice is between baseball and "not-baseball" (the art gallery or concert). If baseball is *not* chosen, the second vote will be between the remaining two options, the art gallery and the concert.

Larry will triumph under such an agenda. In effect, Larry has managed to have his option chosen by first defeating the most-popular Condorcet winner, baseball, with a coalition of less-favored options. *See* Levine & Plott, Agenda Influence and Its Implications, 63 Va.L.Rev. 561, 581 (1977) (reporting results of an actual experiment in which authors imposed their preferences upon their recreational club by arranging agenda to defeat Condorcet winner in favor of program preferred by authors).

5. Another fashion in which voters can manipulate the results of majority voting is to misrepresent their preferences strategically. Suppose that Larry, Curly, and Mo have the preferences diagrammed in Question 4 above. If, in a vote between baseball and the concert, Larry votes for the concert even though he really prefers baseball, baseball will lose to the concert. Then, in a subsequent vote between the art gallery and the concert, art will win.

Question: Arrows' Theorem assumes that such strategic misrepresentation will not occur. Which one of Arrow's five conditions—transitivity, the Pareto postulate, range, nondictatorship, or the independence of irrelevant alternatives—is violated by strategic voting?

6. Agenda-setting may help explain the relative stability of legislative decisions. Consider the example of decisionmaking in the U.S. House of Representatives.

Any Representative may submit proposed legislation. The House Speaker routinely refers such bills to the relevant standing committee charged with examining legislation on that particular subject. When more than one committee has jurisdiction, the Speaker may order sequential referral, *i.e.,* may determine the order in which relevant committees consider a bill.

Once a bill is "in committee," the Committee Chair has the power to schedule hearings on the bill, refer it to a (potentially hostile) subcommittee, or simply let the matter languish. In the U.S. Congress, approximately 80% to 90% of all proposed bills "die in committee." A majority vote of the committee's members is necessary to override the Chair's decision to kill a bill by placing it on the Committee's agenda. The Chair retains the power to determine the order in which the Committee considers particular issues and amendments to the bill.

After the committee has "marked up" the bill to its satisfaction, it is sent to the House floor. At this point, the House Rules Committee determines when the bill shall be considered, how much debate will be allowed, and most particularly whether consideration will be "open rule" (floor amendments permitted), "closed rule" (no floor amendments), or "modified closed rule" (only specified floor amendments allowed). After debate and possible amendment, the entire House votes the bill up or down, usually by a majority vote.

Of course, once the bill is approved, it must be sent to the Senate for approval. If the Senate does not agree with the bill, the two Houses begin reconciliation procedures designed to come up with a proposal which can be approved by a majority of both houses. Once both houses agree on a reconciled bill, it must be presented to the President for signature or veto. See W. Eskridge & P. Frickey, Cases and Materials on Legislation: Statutes and the Creation of Public Policy 28–36 (1988).

> *Questions:* What opportunities for agenda control does such a system create? In particular, which individuals or groups have the greatest power to control the outcome of voting, and how? Is the system rigged to favor changes in legislation or the status quo?

Arrow's Theorem proves that social choices can be intransitive under any decisionmaking rule characterized by the Pareto postulate, nondictatorship, free range of choice, and the independence of irrelevant alternatives. If one or more of those conditions is dropped, Arrow's Theorem no longer applies. The questions following *Kramer,* above, explored how logrolling (which violates the independence of irrelevant alternatives) leads to stable results and greater accuracy in measuring social preference. Tashjian v. Republican Party of Connecticut illustrates what happens when another of Arrow's conditions is violated—the condition of "free range of choice."

The condition of free range requires that individuals may rank alternatives in any order they choose. A person may prefer tennis to skiing and skiing to swimming; she may also prefer skiing to swimming and swimming to tennis. Any kind of ordering of preferences is possible.

On many issues, the preferences of individuals choosing among three or more alternatives do seem to be free ranging. On other issues, however, individuals' preferences seem to fall into a "natural" ordering. Suppose someone is trying to choose among three alternative positions on abortion: (a) abortions should never be permitted; (b) abortion should be allowed only in cases of rape or incest; and (c) abortion should be available on demand. The person choosing may rank those alternatives $a > b > c$, or she may rank them $b > c > a$. It seems implausible, however, that she would rank them $a > c > b$. Someone whose first choice is a total ban on abortions is unlikely to prefer abortion on demand to allowing abortion only in cases of rape or incest.

On some issues, like abortion, preferences seem to form a "spectrum" of positions. Each individual has a favorite point on the spectrum. The closer any given alternative is to that optimum, the more the individual prefers it. Public choice scholars refer to preferences that are not free-ranging but have a natural ordering as "single-peaked." To understand the derivation of that term, note that if options lie along a spectrum from one extreme to another, people with single-peaked preferences will not prefer both extremes over the middle. If the middle is least preferred (a > c > b), the ordering is free-ranging or multipeaked; the two ends of the spectrum are higher than the middle, a valley with two peaks. The plausible abortion orderings are single-peaked, with the middle being the peak (b > c > a) or one of the extremes being the highest point on the peak (a > b > c), as illustrated in Figure 1.

Figure 1

Single and Multipeaked Preferences

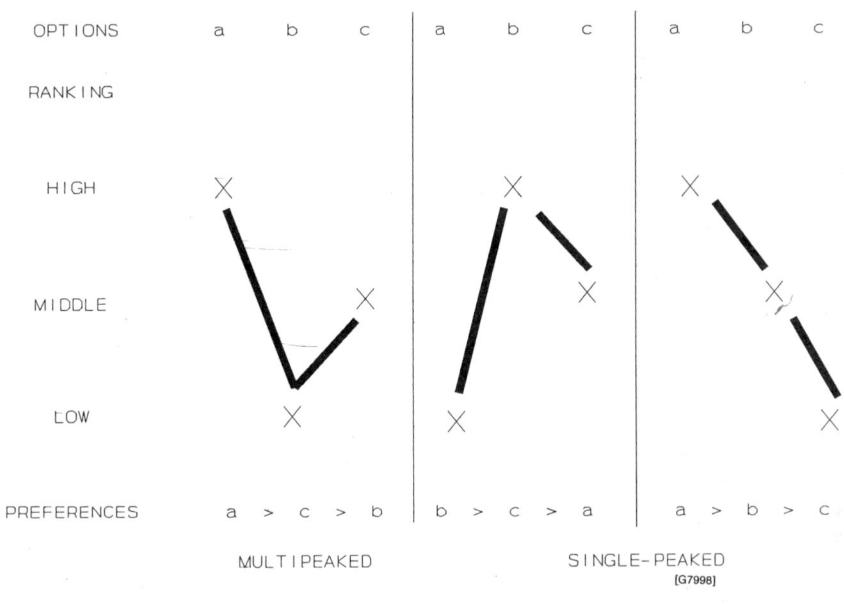

The following case explores the implications of single-peaked preferences for the accuracy and stability of majority voting.

TASHJIAN v. REPUBLICAN PARTY OF CONNECTICUT

Supreme Court of the United States, 1986.
479 U.S. 208, 107 S.Ct. 544, 93 L.Ed.2d 514.

MARSHALL, JUSTICE.

Appellee Republican Party of the State of Connecticut (the Party) in 1984 adopted a party rule which permits independent voters—

registered voters not affiliated with any political party—to vote in Republican primaries for federal and state-wide offices. Appellant Julia Tashjian, the Secretary of the State of Connecticut, is charged with the administration of the State's election statutes, which include a provision requiring voters in any party primary to be registered members of that party. Conn.Gen.Stat. § 9–431 (1985). Appellees, who in addition to the Party include the Party's federal officeholders and the Party's state chairman, challenged this eligibility provision on the ground that it deprives the Party of its First Amendment right to enter into political association with individuals of its own choosing. * * *

* * *

* * * Motivated in part by the demographic importance of independent voters in Connecticut politics * * * [the Republican Party] adopted the Party rule now at issue, which provides:

> "Any elector enrolled as a member of the Republican Party and any elector not enrolled as a member of a party shall be eligible to vote in primaries for nomination of candidates for the offices of United States Senator, United States Representative, Governor, Lieutenant Governor, Secretary of the State, Attorney General, Comptroller and Treasurer."

During the 1984 session, the Republican leadership in the [Connecticut] state legislature, in response to the conflict between the newly enacted Party rule and § 9–431, proposed to amend the statute to allow independents to vote in primaries when permitted by Party rules. The proposed legislation was defeated, substantially along party lines, in both houses of the legislature, which at that time were controlled by the Democratic Party.

The Party and the individual appellees then commenced this action in the District Court, seeking a declaration that § 9–431 infringes the appellees' right to freedom of association for the advancement of common political objectives guaranteed by the First and Fourteenth Amendments, and injunctive relief against its further enforcement. * * *

* * *

The Party here contends that § 9–431 impermissibly burdens the right of its members to determine for themselves with whom they will associate, and whose support they will seek, in their quest for political success. The Party's attempt to broaden the base of public participation in and support for its activities is conduct undeniably central to the exercise of the right of association. * * *

* * *

* * * The statute here places limits upon the group of registered voters whom the Party may invite to participate in the "basic function" of selecting the Party's candidates. The State thus limits the Party's

associational opportunities at the crucial juncture at which the appeal to common principles may be translated into concerted action, and hence to political power in the community.

* * *

Appellant contends that § 9–431 is a narrowly tailored regulation which advances the State's compelling interests * * *.

* * *

[Appellant argues] that the closed primary system avoids voter confusion. Appellant contends that "[t]he legislature could properly find that it would be difficult for the general public to understand what a candidate stood for who was nominated in part by an unknown amorphous body outside the party, while nevertheless using the party name." Appellees respond that the State is attempting to act as the ideological guarantor of the Republican Party's candidates, ensuring that voters are not misled by a "Republican" candidate who professes something other than what the State regards as true Republican principles.

* * *

In arguing that the Party rule interferes with educated decisions by voters, appellant [disregards] the substantial benefit which the Party rule provides to the Party and its members in seeking to choose successful candidates. Given the numerical strength of independent voters in the State, one of the questions most likely to occur to Connecticut Republicans in selecting candidates for public office is, how can the Party most effectively appeal to the independent voter? By inviting independents to assist in the choice at the polls between primary candidates selected at the Party convention, the Party rule is intended to produce the candidate and platform most likely to achieve that goal. The state statute is said to decrease voter confusion, yet it deprives the Party and its members of the opportunity to inform themselves as to the level of support for the Party's candidates among a critical group of electors. * * * The State's legitimate interests in preventing voter confusion and providing for educated and responsible voter decisions in no respect "make it necessary to burden the [Party's] rights."

Finally, appellant contends that § 9–431 furthers the State's compelling interest in protecting the integrity of the two-party system and the responsibility of party government. Appellant argues vigorously and at length that the closed primary system chosen by the state legislature promotes responsiveness by elected officials and strengthens the effectiveness of the political parties.

* * *

Under these circumstances, the views of the State, which to some extent represent the views of the one political party transiently enjoying majority power, as to the optimum methods for preserving party integrity lose much of their force. The State argues that its statute is well designed to save the Republican Party from undertaking a course of conduct destructive of its own interests. But on this point "even if the State were correct, a State, or a court, may not constitutionally substitute its own judgment for that of the Party." The Party's determination of the boundaries of its own association, and of the structure which best allows it to pursue its political goals, is protected by the Constitution. * * *

We conclude that the State's enforcement, under these circumstances, of its closed primary system burdens the First Amendment rights of the Party. The interests which the appellant adduces in support of the statute are insubstantial, and accordingly the statute, as applied to the Party in this case, is unconstitutional.

* * *

Notes and Questions

1. Voter preferences for candidates for political office may be single-peaked if candidates are viewed as falling on a spectrum from radical left through liberal to moderate to conservative to ultra-conservative. Whatever the voter's favorite point on that spectrum, the further a candidate departs from that optimum, the less desirable she will be. A voter is unlikely to prefer a conservative candidate to a liberal and a liberal to a moderate.

Arrow's Theorem predicts that when preferences are multipeaked (free-ranging), majority voting can produce cycling results. That is no longer true when preferences are single-peaked. Suppose Larry, Curly and Mo are voting on candidates for office. Their choices are a liberal (L), a conservative (C), and a middle-of-the-road moderate (M). Conservative Curly prefers C > M > L; Leftist Larry prefers L > M > C; and Muddled Mo prefers M > C > L.

Questions: What happens when the friends vote first between L and C, and then the winner goes up against M? Choose first between M and C, and the winner goes against L? Choose first between L and M, and the winner goes against C?

2. In *Tashjian,* the Republican party challenged a Connecticut statute precluding independents from voting in Republican primaries. The Party claimed that the statute burdened its fundamental freedom of association and harmed its chances of political success through broadening its base of public support.

Question: How did the Republican Party expect to benefit from allowing independents to vote in its primary?

3. United States politics is a two-party system; winning candidates tend to be either Democrats or Republicans. Consider the campaign strategies of two political candidates, one a liberal Democrat (D), and the other a conservative Republican (R). D and R both believe that voter preferences in campaign elections tend to be single-peaked, falling in a continuum between the far left and the far right as illustrated below.

Voters' Political Preferences

D	M	R
Left	(50%)	Right

"M" is the median of voter preferences. Exactly 50% of the electorate have a political philosophy more liberal than the median (to the left of M); 50% have a more conservative philosophy (to the right of M). Thus, M represents the preferences of the median voter.

Before the election, the political philosophies of D and R lie to the left and to the right, respectively, of the median position. However, both D and R realize that to win the election they must put together a campaign platform that attracts the support of more than half of all voters. Voters with philosophies more conservative than R's are sure to vote for R over D, just as voters who lie to the left of D are trapped into picking D over R. But to win, D or R must capture the votes of the individuals whose political philosophies lie between them. In particular, each candidate must try to capture the "median" voter whose vote puts the candidate over the 50% threshold of victory.

Questions: How will the need to gain the support of the median voter affect the political position each candidate is likely to espouse? Why are two-party system politics dominated by the median voter's preferences?

4. When the conditions of Arrow's Theorem apply, majority voting can produce cycling results. This not only implies that the results of majority voting may be unstable, but also raises serious doubt about the accuracy of majority voting as a means of weighing social preferences.

When voter preferences are single-peaked, Arrow's Theorem is inapplicable and voting produces a stable outcome. But stability is not necessarily accuracy.

Question: A voting system is accurate when it produces social choices that maximize social welfare or utility. Are single-peaked preferences sufficient to ensure that the outcome of majority voting is accurate as well as stable?

5. In *Tashjian,* the State argued that closed primaries are essential to "protect the integrity of the two-party system." Previous questions suggest that an open primary tempts both parties to appeal to the political preferences of the median voter.

Question: How do closed primaries contribute to preserving two distinct parties with two distinct political platforms?

6. When voter preferences are single-peaked, majority voting produces stable outcomes determined by the median voter. The legislative branch of the United States government involves two types of voting. Citizens vote in general elections to choose representatives to the legislature, and representatives in turn vote on particular pieces of legislation. Question 1 suggested that if candidates for the legislature fall on an ideological spectrum from left to right, citizens' preferences in general elections are likely to be single-peaked.

Question: Is the assumption that voter's preferences in general elections are single-peaked sensible given the phenomenon of "single-issue" candidates who put particular emphasis on issues such as abortion or gun control?

7. Representatives chosen in general elections themselves vote on proposed statutes in the legislature. Most state constitutions contain a provision to the effect that proposed legislation must address a single subject. For example, the Minnesota Constitution provides that "No law shall embrace more than one subject, which shall be expressed in its title." Minn. Const. Art. IV, § 27 (1857). Such requirements effectively preclude the passage of omnibus bills on a number of unrelated matters. In contrast, the U.S. Congress permits omnibus bills.

Question: What are the implications of single-subject and omnibus bills for the stability of legislative voting?

b. Wealth Redistribution Under Majority Rule

The public choice analysis of voting has assumed thus far that the coercive state's goal is identifying and pursuing policies that efficiently improve its citizens' well-being. Under a rule of unanimity rational citizens are unlikely to agree to anything else. Under majority rule, however, the state's coercive power can be turned to satisfying the desires of a segment of society rather than the collective needs of all.

The Framers of the U. S. Constitution were sensitive to the possibility that a legislature governed by majority rule might serve the interests of part of society rather than the whole. Consider Article I of the Constitution, which provides:

> Representatives and direct Taxes shall be apportioned among the several States which may be included within this Union, according to their respective Numbers, which shall be determined * * * within three Years after the first Meeting of the Congress of the United States, and within every subsequent Term of Ten Years * * * .

In 1894, after lengthy and heated debate, Congress imposed a 2% tax on individual and corporate income from real property, personal property such as stocks or bonds, and business or employment. Shortly after the tax statute became effective, the Supreme Court agreed to hear *Pollock v. Farmer's Loan & Trust Co.,* in which a corporate shareholder sought to enjoin his corporation from paying the income tax on the ground that the tax was unconstitutional under Article I.

POLLOCK v. FARMERS' LOAN & TRUST COMPANY

Supreme Court of the United States, 1895.
157 U.S. 429, 15 S.Ct. 673, 39 L.Ed. 759.

FULLER, CHIEF JUSTICE.

* * *

The contention of the complainant is:

First. That the law in question, in imposing a tax on the income or rents of real estate, imposes a tax upon the real estate itself; and in imposing a tax on the interest or other income of bonds or other personal property, held for the purposes of income or ordinarily yielding income, imposes a tax upon the personal estate itself; that such tax is a direct tax, and void because imposed without regard to the rule of apportionment; and that by reason thereof the whole law is invalidated.

* * *

The constitution provides that representatives and direct taxes shall be apportioned among the several States according to numbers, and that no direct tax shall be laid except according to the enumeration provided for * * *.

The men who framed and adopted that instrument had just emerged from the struggle for independence whose rallying cry had been that "taxation and representation go together."

The mother country had taught the colonists, in the contests waged to establish that taxes could not be imposed by the sovereign except as they were granted by the representatives of the realm, that self-taxation constituted the main security against oppression. * * * The principle was that the consent of those who were expected to pay it was essential to the validity of any tax.

The States were about, for all national purposes embraced in the Constitution, to become one, united under the same sovereign authority, and governed by the same laws. But as they still retained their jurisdiction over all persons and things within their territorial limits * * * they were careful to see to it that taxation and representation should go together, so that the sovereignty reserved should not be impaired, and that when congress, and especially the house of representatives, where it was specifically provided that all revenue bills must originate, voted a tax upon property, it should be with the consciousness, and under the responsibility, that in so doing the tax so voted would proportionately fall upon the immediate constituents of those who imposed it.

* * * All the thirteen were Seaboard States, but they varied in maritime importance, and differences existed between them in population, in wealth, in the character of property and of business interests. * * *

* * *

Nothing can be clearer than that what the Constitution intended to guard against was the exercise by the general government of the power of directly taxing persons and property within any State through a majority made up from the other States. It is true that the effect of requiring direct taxes to be apportioned among the States in proportion to their population is necessarily that the amount of taxes on the individual taxpayer in a State having the taxable subject-matter to a larger extent in proportion to its population than another State has, would be less than in such other State, but this inequality must be held to have been contemplated, and was manifestly designed to operate to restrain the exercise of the power of direct taxation to extraordinary emergencies, and to prevent an attack upon accumulated property by mere force of numbers.

* * *

* * * [T]he acceptance of the rule of apportionment was one of the compromises which made the adoption of the Constitution possible, and secured the creation of that dual form of government, so elastic and so strong, which has thus far survived in unabated vigor. If, by calling a tax indirect when it is essentially direct, the rule of protection could be frittered away, one of the great landmarks defining the boundary between the Nation and the States of which it is composed, would have disappeared, and with it one of the bulwarks of private rights and private property.

We are of opinion that the law in question, so far as it levies a tax on the rents or income of real estate, is [an unapportioned direct tax] in violation of the Constitution, and is invalid.

* * *

Notes and Questions

1. Whether a particular tax is a direct tax that must be apportioned among the states in proportion to their census population or is "indirect" may be far from obvious. Case law on the question shows confusion. See Hylton v. United States, 3 U.S. (3 Dall.) 171, 1 L.Ed. 556 (1796) (annual tax on carriages held indirect); Springer v. United States, 102 U.S. (12 Otto) 586, 26 L.Ed. 253 (1880) (Civil War income tax upheld as indirect); see generally 1 Bittker, Federal Taxation of Income, Estates and Gifts ¶ 1.2.2 (1981) (discussing difficulty of determining what is direct tax under Constitution). In *Pollock,* the Supreme Court concluded that a tax on income from real estate was equivalent to a direct tax on the real estate itself and was unconstitutional unless apportioned among the states according to their census populations.

2. According to Chief Justice Fuller, Article I was intended to guard against "the exercise by the general government of the power of directly taxing persons and property within any state through a majority made up from the other states" or "an attack upon accumulated property by mere force of numbers." Fuller observed that the original thirteen colonies differed substantially "in population, in wealth, [and] in the character of property and of business interests."

Questions: Under majority rule, how can interstate differences in wealth, property and population lead to taxes that redistribute wealth from one state to another? The Constitution provides two protections against disparate taxation: the Apportionment Clause, and the requirement that tax legislation originate in the House of Representatives rather than the Senate. How do those provisions discourage redistributive taxation?

3. The possibility that a coercive government may transfer wealth rather than create it suggests another explanation for the state; the state may exist because one subgroup in society wants to exploit the remainder.

Questions: How does the wealth-transfer theory of the state compare with contractarian theory premised on citizen consent to state coercion? Consider Justice Fuller's claim in *Pollock* that "the consent of those who [are] expected to pay it [is] essential to the validity of any tax." Which model best describes British government of the American colonies in the late eighteenth century?

4. In a subsequent opinion in *Pollock,* the Supreme Court held that the unconstitutional provisions of the income tax statute rendered the statute invalid as a whole. See Pollock v. Farmer's Loan & Trust Co., 158 U.S. 601, 634–35, 15 S.Ct. 912, 919–20, 39 L.Ed. 1108 (1895). Again writing for the majority, Chief Justice Fuller noted:

> If it be true that the Constitution should have been so framed that a tax of this kind could be laid, the instrument defines the way for its amendment. In no part of it was greater sagacity displayed. Except that no state, without its consent, can be deprived of its equal suffrage in the Senate, the Constitution may be amended upon the concurrence of two-thirds of both houses, and the ratification of the legislatures or conventions of the several States, or through a Federal convention when applied for by the legislatures of two-thirds of the States, and upon like ratification.

The Sixteenth Amendment authorizing a federal income tax without apportionment was ratified in 1913.

Question: How do the requirements of two-thirds Congressional concurrence and ratification by three-fourths of the states decrease the likelihood that a federal tax would redistribute wealth among the states in a fashion that did not increase overall utility?

5. The modern Internal Revenue Code provides for "progressive" income taxation. Individuals' *proportionate* tax burdens increase with income. For example, a progressive tax system might impose no tax on the first $10,000 an individual earns, impose a 10% tax on the next $10,000, take 20% of the third $10,000 earned, and so forth. Even a flat-rate system requires high-income individuals to pay more taxes than persons with low incomes. But the wealthy bear an even larger share of the tax burden under progressive taxation.

Assume that tax revenues pay for government services that benefit rich and poor equally. (Question 8, below, reexamines that assumption.) If the government collects more from the rich than the poor but spends those funds on projects that benefit rich and poor equally, government redistributes wealth from the rich to the poor.

Question: Why might all members of society, rich and poor, prefer a progressive income tax? Recall Rawls' arguments in support of the maximin principle discussed earlier.

6. Wealthy individuals moved by pity or empathy for the poor can (and do) give to charities that help the worst-off in society.

Question: If the wealthy have a "taste for charity," why might a coercive progressive income tax serve such altruistic preferences for wealth redistribution more effectively than a voluntary system that permits rich individuals to give when they feel like doing so?

7. A redistributive tax unanimously approved by rich and poor alike meets Pareto's strict criteria for the desirability of a reallocation. The efficiency implications of a redistributive tax imposed by majority rule are less clear.

Questions: Is a progressive tax system favored by a majority consisting of the poor and middle-class, but disfavored by the rich, utility maximizing? Wealth maximizing?

8. Majority rule by definition permits state action that benefits one group (the approving majority) but leaves another (the dissenting minority) worse off. Any action based on less-than-unanimous consent thus potentially involves an element of "redistribution." Majority rule's redistributive possibilities are most obvious when the state takes wealth from (imposes taxes on) a subgroup of society. However, providing disparate benefits can redistribute wealth just as imposing disparate costs does.

Question 5 assumed that the revenues raised under a progressive tax system were spent on projects benefiting rich and poor equally. In reality, government programs often benefit some individuals or groups more than others.

Question: What are the redistributive effects of the following government activities: building a federally-funded "supercollider" research facility in a particular location; imposing strict pollution controls on smokestack industries; creating entitlement programs to provide medical and income-support benefits for low-income individuals; and federally insuring deposits in savings and loan institutions?

9. Because a coercive state can redistribute wealth through both uneven taxation and uneven provision of benefits, both sides of the equation must be considered to calculate the net redistribution of wealth from government action.

Questions: Consider the following three government activities: providing free (but low quality) education at the primary and secondary levels; compulsory vaccination for polio; and maintaining a police force. If those programs are paid for by a poll tax imposed on rich and poor alike, who benefits most and who benefits least from government intervention? If they are paid for by a flat 10% tax on all property? Paid for by a progressive tax system?

10. Any group that hopes to profit by extracting wealth from others under majority rule must put together a redistributing program that benefits (and so has the support of) more than half the individuals entitled to vote on the measure. Once a majority coalition is created, however, there is no reason to try to gain an even larger percentage of support for the redistributive proposal. To the contrary. The greater the percentage of voters who gain from the proposal, the greater the number to share the spoils and the smaller the number to be exploited. A coalition of 51% exploiting the remaining 49% enjoys greater average gains than a coalition

of 95% exploiting the remaining 5%. Thus individuals who hope for the maximum gain from redistribution under majority rule will put together the *minimum winning coalition* necessary to pass the measure under whatever voting rule applies. See W.H. Riker, The Theory of Political Coalitions (1962).

Bargaining among potential coalition members can destabilize redistributive coalitions. Suppose Poor Peter, Rich Richard and Middle-Class Mary buy a lottery ticket together and are thrilled when they win $300. They agree to divide the winnings according to majority rule. Poor Peter proposes that he get the entire $300. Not surprisingly, Richard and Mary form a coalition and propose that Peter receive nothing and they receive $150 each. Peter, trying to make the best out of a bad situation, approaches Richard and offers to form a coalition under which Richard will get $200, Peter will get $100, and Mary will receive nothing. When Mary finds out she also approaches Richard and suggests that Richard get $201, she get $99, and Peter get nothing. At this point Peter approaches Mary and suggests a coalition under which Peter gets $200, Mary gets $100, and Richard gets nothing—a deal that gives Mary more than the coalition she is trying to form with Richard.

When redistributive coalitions are unstable, it is difficult for one group in society systematically to exploit another. Calculations of the overall amount of wealth redistribution resulting from all government programs in the United States in 1984 indicate that, while the direction of redistribution was generally from the rich to the poor, the amount involved was fairly small. See D. Mueller, Public Choice II 453, Table 23.2 (1989).

C. RENT-SEEKING AND THE ECONOMIC THEORY OF LEGISLATION

Thus far we have assumed that government's goal is improving society's welfare (whether measured in utility or wealth) by controlling excessive external costs and other market failures. The preceding discussion suggests that the state may fail to achieve that end when majority voting proves an inaccurate means of identifying and measuring social preferences, or permits one group in society to exploit the remainder. This section considers a second obstacle to efficient government intervention—the self-interested, rational maximizing behavior of the individual voters and elected representatives who comprise the political state.

HARPER v. VIRGINIA BOARD OF ELECTIONS

Supreme Court of the United States, 1966.
383 U.S. 663, 86 S.Ct. 1079, 16 L.Ed.2d 169.

DOUGLAS, JUSTICE.

These are suits by Virginia residents to have declared unconstitutional Virginia's poll tax. * * *

* * *

Long ago in *Yick Wo v. Hopkins,* the Court referred to "the political franchise of voting" as a "fundamental political right, because preservative of all rights." Recently in *Reynolds v. Sims,* we said, "Undoubtedly, the right of suffrage is a fundamental matter in a free and democratic society. Especially since the right to exercise the franchise in a free and unimpaired manner is preservative of other basic civil and political rights, any alleged infringement of the right of citizens to vote must be carefully and meticulously scrutinized." * * *

It is argued that a State may exact fees from citizens for many different kinds of licenses; that if it can demand from all an equal fee for a driver's license, it can demand from all an equal poll tax for voting. But we must remember that the interest of the State, when it comes to voting, is limited to the power to fix qualifications. Wealth, like race, creed, or color, is not germane to one's ability to participate intelligently in the electoral process. * * * To introduce wealth or payment of a fee as a measure of a voter's qualifications is to introduce a capricious or irrelevant factor. The degree of the discrimination is irrelevant. In this context—that is, as a condition of obtaining a ballot—the requirement of fee paying causes an "invidious" discrimination that runs afoul of the Equal Protection Clause. * * *

* * *

We have long been mindful that where fundamental rights and liberties are asserted under the Equal Protection Clause, classifications which might invade or restrain them must be closely scrutinized and carefully confined.

Those principles apply here. For to repeat, wealth or fee paying has, in our view, no relation to voting qualifications; the right to vote is too precious, too fundamental to be so burdened or conditioned.

Reversed.

HARLAN, JUSTICE, dissenting.

* * *

The Equal Protection Clause prevents States from arbitrarily treating people differently under their laws. Whether any such differing treatment is to be deemed arbitrary depends on whether or not it reflects an appropriate differentiating classification among those affected; the clause has never been thought to require equal treatment of all persons despite differing circumstances. The test evolved by this Court for determining whether an asserted justifying classification exists is whether such a classification can be deemed to be founded on some rational and otherwise constitutionally permissible state policy. * * * This standard reduces to a minimum the likelihood that the federal judiciary will judge state policies in terms of the individual notions and predilections of its own members, and until recently it has been followed in all kinds of "equal protection" cases.

* * *

* * * Is there a rational basis for Virginia's poll tax as a voting qualification? I think the answer to that question is undoubtedly "yes."

* * *

* * * [I]t is certainly a rational argument that payment of some minimal poll tax promotes civic responsibility, weeding out those who do not care enough about public affairs to pay $1.50 or thereabouts a year for the exercise of the franchise. It is also arguable, indeed it was probably accepted as sound political theory by a large percentage of Americans through most of our history, that people with some property have a deeper stake in community affairs, and are consequently more responsible, more educated, more knowledgeable, more worthy of confidence, than those without means, and that the community and Nation would be better managed if the franchise were restricted to such citizens. * * *

* * *

I would affirm the decision of the District Court.

Notes and Questions

1. Both the majority and the minority opinions in *Harper* apparently assumed that a $1.50 poll tax would deter at least a few voters from voting. The theory seems to be that voting becomes less attractive when the costs of voting are increased. One study has shown that a $6.00 poll tax imposed in 1960 did, indeed, reduce the average individual's probability of voting by 42%. See Ashenfelter & Kelley, Determinants of Participation in Presidential Elections, 18 J. L. & Econ. 695, 698 (1975).

Harlan's dissent argued that Virginia's poll tax was intended to discourage certain citizens from voting as much as to raise revenue. Among the persons likely to be discouraged from voting were the poor (who Harlan suggested might not have as deep a stake in the community) and the indifferent (who do not care deeply about exercising their franchise).

Questions: Does the absence of a poll tax mean that voting is a costless activity? What other costs are associated with voting? Are those burdens greater for the rich or the poor?

2. A rational voter will vote only if the costs of doing so are less than the benefits.

Question: Given that voting imposes costs, what are its benefits?

3. Applying the model of rational maximization to why voters vote raises a quandary known as the *paradox of voting.* If individuals vote to affect election outcomes, any rational voter should realize quickly that the odds of her vote making a difference in results are negligible. The benefit of voting is therefore the expected difference in the voter's utility from electing one candidate over another, multiplied by the infinitesimal chance that the voter's vote will determine which candidate wins. At the same time, voting involves significant costs in terms of time, money, and inconvenience. For the average person, any possible net benefit from voting is

substantially outweighed by the risk the voter will be run down by a truck on the way to the polls.

The paradox of voting suggests that it is irrational for the average person to vote. See A. Downs, An Economic Theory of Democracy 11–14 (1957). Nevertheless, many individuals who appear rational vote regularly. Some economists speculate that people have a "taste for voting" so that voting, as political participation, provides utility even when voters have no real expectation that their vote will make a difference to the election's outcome.

4. Suppose individuals vote only to influence outcome. In that case, very few indeed might bother to vote.

Questions: How might very low voter turnout affect a rational maximizer's decision whether or not to vote? Does it matter how close the vote is likely to be, that is, whether the election is hotly contested or has a clear frontrunner?

5. Consider Justice Harlan's argument that poll taxes "[weed] out those who do not care enough about public affairs to pay $1.50 or thereabouts a year for the exercise of the franchise."

Questions: How might a poll tax improve voting's ability to assist the state in maximizing utility? Wealth?

6. In some states and municipalities citizens occasionally vote directly on referenda addressing specific government policies. Most often, however, citizens express their policy preferences by electing representatives to state and federal legislatures charged with the authority to make law. It seems reasonable to assume that representatives, like the voters who elect them, are self-interested rational maximizers. That raises the risk that representatives will vote in a fashion that ignores their constituents' interests but furthers the representatives' personal goals.

The voter who wishes to guard against a representative's running amok must first investigate candidates for office to select the candidate most likely to vote in accord with the voter's preferences and then monitor the candidate's voting record after election to ensure that the representative is, in fact, furthering the voter's interests.

Questions: Given the uncertain benefits of voting, how much effort is the rational voter likely to spend educating herself on candidates' positions and overseeing elected representatives' voting performance? On what sources of information are rational voters likely to rely in selecting and monitoring representatives?

BUCKLEY v. VALEO

Supreme Court of the United States, 1976.
424 U.S. 1, 96 S.Ct. 612, 46 L.Ed.2d 659.

PER CURIAM.

These appeals present constitutional challenges to the key provisions of the Federal Election Campaign Act of 1971 (Act) * * *.

* * *

* * * The major contribution and expenditure limitations in the Act prohibit individuals from contributing more than $25,000 in a single year or more than $1,000 to any single candidate for an election campaign and from spending more than $1,000 a year "relative to a clearly identified candidate." Other provisions * * * limit the overall amount that can be spent by a candidate in campaigning for federal office.

* * *

The Act's contribution and expenditure limitations operate in an area of the most fundamental First Amendment activities. Discussion of public issues and debate on the qualifications of candidates are integral to the operation of the system of government established by our Constitution. * * * In a republic where the people are sovereign, the ability of the citizenry to make informed choices among candidates for office is essential, for the identities of those who are elected will inevitably shape the course that we follow as a nation. * * *

* * *

A restriction on the amount of money a person or group can spend on political communication during a campaign necessarily reduces the quantity of expression by restricting the number of issues discussed, the depth of their exploration, and the size of the audience reached. This is because virtually every means of communicating ideas in today's mass society requires the expenditure of money. The distribution of the humblest handbill or leaflet entails printing, paper, and circulation costs. Speeches and rallies generally necessitate hiring a hall and publicizing the event. The electorate's increasing dependence on television, radio, and other mass media for news and information has made these expensive modes of communication indispensable instruments of effective political speech.

* * *

By contrast with a limitation upon expenditures for political expression, a limitation upon the amount that any one person or group may contribute to a candidate or political committee entails only a marginal restriction upon the contributor's ability to engage in free communication. A contribution serves as a general expression of support for the candidate and his views, but does not communicate the underlying basis for the support. The quantity of communication by the contributor does not increase perceptibly with the size of his contribution, since the expression rests solely on the undifferentiated, symbolic act of contributing. At most, the size of the contribution provides a very rough index of the intensity of the contributor's support for the candidate. A limitation on the amount of money a person may give to a candidate or campaign organization thus involves little direct restraint on his political communication * * *.

* * *

Appellees argue that the Act's restrictions on large campaign contributions are justified by three governmental interests. According to the parties and *amici,* the primary interest served by the limitations and, indeed, by the Act as a whole, is the prevention of corruption and the appearance of corruption spawned by the real or imagined coercive influence of large financial contributions on candidates' positions and on their actions if elected to office. Two "ancillary" interests underlying the Act are also allegedly furthered by the $1,000 limits on contributions. First, the limits serve to mute the voices of affluent persons and groups in the election process and thereby to equalize the relative ability of all citizens to affect the outcome of elections. Second, it is argued, the ceilings may to some extent act as a brake on the skyrocketing cost of political campaigns and thereby serve to open the political system more widely to candidates without access to sources of large amounts of money.

It is unnecessary to look beyond the Act's primary purpose—to limit the actuality and appearance of corruption resulting from large individual financial contributions—in order to find a constitutionally sufficient justification for the $1,000 contribution limitation. Under a system of private financing of elections, a candidate lacking immense personal or family wealth must depend on financial contributions from others to provide the resources necessary to conduct a successful campaign. The increasing importance of the communications media and sophisticated mass-mailing and polling operations to effective campaigning make the raising of large sums of money an ever more essential ingredient of an effective candidacy. To the extent that large contributions are given to secure a political *quid pro quo* from current and potential office holders, the integrity of our system of representative democracy is undermined. * * *

* * *

We find that, under the rigorous standard of review established by our prior decisions, the weighty interests served by restricting the size of financial contributions to political candidates are sufficient to justify the limited effect upon First Amendment freedoms caused by the $1,000 contribution ceiling.

* * *

The Act's expenditure ceilings impose direct and substantial restraints on the quantity of political speech. The most drastic of the limitations restricts individuals and groups, including political parties that fail to place a candidate on the ballot, to an expenditure of $1,000 "relative to a clearly identified candidate during a calendar year." * * *

* * *

We find that the governmental interest in preventing corruption and the appearance of corruption is inadequate to justify [the] ceiling on independent expenditures [relative to a clearly identified candidate]. * * *

* * *

It is argued, however, that the ancillary governmental interest in equalizing the relative ability of individuals and groups to influence the outcome of elections serves to justify the limitation on express advocacy of the election or defeat of candidates imposed by [the independent] expenditure ceiling. But the concept that government may restrict the speech of some elements of our society in order to enhance the relative voice of others is wholly foreign to the First Amendment, which was designed "to secure 'the widest possible dissemination of information from diverse and antagonistic sources,'" and "'to assure unfettered interchange of ideas for the bringing about of political and social changes desired by the people.'" The First Amendment's protection against governmental abridgment of free expression cannot properly be made to depend on a person's financial ability to engage in public discussion.

* * *

Section 608(c) places limitations on overall campaign expenditures by candidates seeking nomination for election and election to federal office. Presidential candidates may spend $10,000,000 in seeking nomination for office and an additional $20,000,000 in the general election campaign. The ceiling on senatorial campaigns is pegged to the size of the voting-age population of the State with minimum dollar amounts applicable to campaigns in States with small populations. * * * The Act imposes blanket $70,000 limitations on both primary campaigns and general election campaigns for the House of Representatives * * *

No governmental interest that has been suggested is sufficient to justify the restriction on the quantity of political expression imposed by § 608(c)'s campaign expenditure limitations. * * *

* * *

The campaign expenditure ceilings appear to be designed primarily to serve the governmental interests in reducing the allegedly skyrocketing costs of political campaigns. * * * [T]he mere growth in the cost of federal election campaigns in and of itself provides no basis for governmental restrictions on the quantity of campaign spending and the resulting limitation on the scope of federal campaigns. The First Amendment denies government the power to determine that spending to promote one's political views is wasteful, excessive, or unwise. * * *

In sum, the provisions of the Act that impose a $1,000 limitation on contributions to a single candidate, a $5,000 limitation on contributions by a political committee to a single candidate, and a $25,000 limitation on total contributions by an individual during any calendar year, are constitutionally valid. These limitations * * * constitute the Act's primary weapons against the reality or appearance of improper influence stemming from the dependence of candidates on large campaign contributions. The contribution ceilings thus serve the basic governmental interest in safeguarding the integrity of the electoral process without directly impinging upon the rights of individual citizens and candidates to engage in political debate and discussion. By contrast, the First Amendment requires the invalidation of the Act's independent expenditure ceiling * * * and its ceilings on overall campaign expenditures. These provisions place substantial and direct restrictions on the ability of candidates, citizens, and associations to engage in protected political expression, restrictions that the First Amendment cannot tolerate.

* * *

Affirmed in part and reversed in part.

WHITE, JUSTICE, concurring in part and dissenting in part.

* * *

* * * [I dissent] from the Court's view that the expenditure limitations * * * violate the First Amendment.

* * *

I have little doubt * * * that limiting the total that can be spent will ease the candidate's understandable obsession with fundraising, and so free him and his staff to communicate in more places and ways unconnected with the fundraising function. There is nothing objectionable—indeed it seems to me a weighty interest in favor of the provision—in the attempt to insulate the political expression of federal candidates from the influence inevitably exerted by the endless job of raising increasingly large sums of money. I regret that the Court has returned them all to the treadmill.

It is also important to restore and maintain public confidence in federal elections. It is critical to obviate or dispel the impression that federal elections are purely and simply a function of money, that federal offices are bought and sold or that political races are reserved for those who have the facility—and the stomach—for doing whatever it takes to bring together those interests, groups, and individuals that can raise or contribute large fortunes in order to prevail at the polls.

* * *

Notes and Questions

1. To understand the consequences of representatives' self-interest for legislative voting, one must form a theory of what representatives desire. Among representatives' many likely sources of utility is election itself. Campaigning for political office involves substantial time, effort, and risk of failure. No rational individual would incur such costs unless she expected to derive utility from election.

Both the majority opinion in *Buckley* and Justice White's dissent noted that campaigning requires large amounts of money. Consider how financing can improve a candidate's likelihood of election. Since it is illegal to buy votes outright, campaign dollars tend to be used to purchase posters, leaflets, campaign buttons, television and radio time, and polling and political consulting services.

Questions: Given the theory of the rational voter developed in the notes following *Harper,* how is advertising likely to affect the rational voter's preferences? How can using the media improve a candidate's chances? Does political advertising improve the accuracy of election outcomes?

2. The fact that political campaigns usually are financed from contributions and that Congress felt compelled to pass legislation limiting such contributions raises interesting economic questions. Not the least is why so many people are trying so hard to give so much money to politicians in the first place. The economist would assume contributors are buying something.

The majority opinion in *Buckley* mentioned two types of goods and services contributors might be trying to purchase. The first, less troubling, reason for contributing to a candidate's campaign is to support "the candidate and his views." If a contributor believed that one candidate's platform would provide her with substantially more utility than the other candidate's platform would, the contributor might find it in her interest to help finance her ideologically-favored candidate's campaign. The second, less attractive, motive is to exert a "coercive influence * * * on candidates' positions and on their actions if elected to office." The first motive seems to presume that candidates want to win elections to implement their preferred policies. The second suggests that candidates choose their policies to woo contributors and win elections.

Both theories suggest that making contributions increases the likelihood that the representative elected will vote in a fashion that serves the contributor's interests. However, the two theories lead to very different predictions for contributor behavior. Consider a contributor trying to decide whether to make campaign contributions to one candidate or to both. Consider also a contributor trying to decide to whether to give a contribution in a very close election or in an election where one candidate is a clear frontrunner.

Question: Which contribution strategy does each theory predict in the two circumstances?

3. If elected representatives cater to big contributors' interests at the expense of their constituents' when voting in the legislature, they run the risk that voters will detect their defection and refuse to reelect them. Accepting contributions is self-defeating if it loses more votes than it gains.

Question: What factors reduce the likelihood that the rational voter will detect that a representative's vote on an issue favors contributors' interests rather than constituents'?

4. The questions following *Kramer* examined how majority voting's accuracy as a measure of social preferences is improved by allowing voters to express their intensity of preference. In the legislature, representatives can express their preference intensity to some extent by "logrolling." However, logrolling is not practicable in general elections where a large population of citizens elects representatives to the legislature.

Question: Although the majority in *Buckley* upheld the limitation on campaign contributions, it noted that "the size of the contribution provides a very rough index of the contributor's support for the candidate." From an economic perspective, isn't such a means of expressing intensity of preference in general elections desirable?

5. In addition to finding that the Federal Election Campaign Act of 1971 (FECA) implicated First Amendment interests in free expression, *Buckley* held that "[t]he Act's contribution and expenditure limitations also impinge on protected associational freedoms. Making a contribution, like joining a political party, serves to affiliate a person with a candidate. In addition, it enables like-minded persons to pool their resources in furtherance of common political goals."

Federal law invites individuals to pool resources in making campaign contributions. While the FECA prohibits individual contributions of more than $1,000 to a individual candidate or $25,000 overall, the statute permits individuals to give up to $5,000 to a political action committee (PAC). PACs in turn are free to contribute up to $5,000 to individual candidates and unlimited amounts overall. The 1970s and 1980s saw a proliferation in the number of PACs and a corresponding increase in their importance to campaign finance. See W. Eskridge and P. Frickey, Legislation: Statutes and the Creation of Public Policy 218–21 (1988).

Concerted group action is common not only at the campaign finance stage but also after election when special interest groups lobby legislators to vote one way or another on particular issues. Lobbyists influence legislative voting both through implied promises of political support and contributions in future campaigns, and by providing selective information to legislators trying to determine which way to vote. Business interests seem particularly likely to form industry-wide groups to lobby on legislation affecting the industry. The American Petroleum Institute (API) and the Motor Vehicles Manufacturers Association (MVMA) are typical examples. However, organizations such as the Sierra Club and the National Rifle Association representing non-business interests lobby as well.

Question: Why might individual persons and businesses find it advantageous to form a group to lobby rather than relying on solitary efforts?

WILLIAMSON v. LEE OPTICAL OF OKLAHOMA

Supreme Court of the United States, 1955.
348 U.S. 483, 75 S.Ct. 461, 99 L.Ed. 563.

DOUGLAS, JUSTICE.

This suit was instituted in the District Court to have an Oklahoma law declared unconstitutional and to enjoin state officials from enforcing it, for the reason that it allegedly violated various provisions of the Federal Constitution. * * *

The District Court held unconstitutional portions of three sections of the Act. First, it held invalid under the Due Process Clause of the Fourteenth Amendment the portions of [the Act] which make it unlawful for any person not a licensed optometrist or opthalmologist to fit lenses to a face or to duplicate or replace into frames lenses or other optical appliances, except upon written prescriptive authority of an Oklahoma licensed opthalmologist or optometrist.

An ophthalmologist is a duly licensed physician who specializes in the care of the eyes. An optometrist examines eyes for refractive error, recognizes (but does not treat) diseases of the eye, and fills prescriptions for eyeglasses. The optician is an artisan qualified to grind lenses, fill prescriptions, and fit frames.

The effect of [the Oklahoma law] is to forbid the optician from fitting or duplicating lenses without a prescription from an ophthalmologist or optometrist. In practical effect, it means that no optician can fit old glasses into new frames or supply a lens, whether it be a new lens or one to duplicate a lost or broken lens, without a prescription. The District Court conceded that it was in the competence of the police power of a State to regulate the examination of the eyes. But it rebelled at the notion that a State could require a prescription from an optometrist or ophthalmologist "to take old lenses and place them in new frames and then fit the completed spectacles to the face of the eyeglass wearer." It held that such a requirement was not "reasonably and rationally related to the health and welfare of the people." The court found that through mechanical devices and ordinary skills the optician could take a broken lens or a fragment thereof, measure its power, and reduce it to prescriptive terms. The court held that "Although on this precise issue of duplication, the legislature in the instant regulation was dealing with a matter of public interest, the particular means chosen are neither reasonably necessary nor reasonably related to the end sought to be achieved." It was, accordingly, the opinion of the court that this provision of the law violated the Due Process Clause by arbitrarily interfering with the optician's right to do business.

* * *

The Oklahoma law may exact a needless, wasteful requirement in many cases. But it is for the legislature, not the courts, to balance the advantages and disadvantages of the new requirement. It appears that in many cases the optician can easily supply the new frames or new lenses without reference to the old written prescription. It also appears that many written prescriptions contain no directive data in regard to fitting spectacles to the face. But in some cases the directions contained in the prescription are essential, if the glasses are to be fitted so as to correct the particular defects of vision or alleviate the eye condition. The legislature might have concluded that the frequency of occasions when a prescription is necessary was sufficient to justify this regulation of the fitting of eyeglasses. Likewise, when it is necessary to duplicate a lens, a written prescription may or may not be necessary. But the legislature might have concluded that one was needed often enough to require one in every case. Or the legislature may have concluded that eye examinations were so critical, not only for correction of vision but also for detection of latent ailments or diseases, that every change in frames and every duplication of a lens should be accompanied by a prescription from a medical expert. To be sure, the present law does not require a new examination of the eyes every time the frames are changed or the lenses duplicated. For if the old prescription is on file with the optician, he can go ahead and make the new fitting or duplicate the lenses. But the law need not be in every respect logically consistent with its aims to be constitutional. It is enough that there is an evil at hand for correction, and that it might be thought that the particular legislative measure was a rational way to correct it.

The day is gone when this Court uses the Due Process Clause of the Fourteenth Amendment to strike down state laws, regulatory of business and industrial conditions, because they may be unwise, improvident, or out of harmony with a particular school of thought. We emphasize again what Chief Justice Waite said in Munn v. Illinois, "For protection against abuses by legislatures the people must resort to the polls, not to the courts."

* * *

Affirmed in part and reversed in part.

Notes and Questions

1. When the state allocates a scarce resource among parties with conflicting claims to that resource, inevitably some parties win and others lose. The scarce resource allocated in *Lee Optical* was the right to sell replacement prescription lenses and eyeglass frames to the public. Two groups pressed claims to that right: the optometrists and the opticians.

The optometrists had much to gain from legislation preventing opticians from providing lenses or frames without a prescription on file. The optometrists' nationwide policy was never to issue a prescription for corrective lenses without insisting that the patient also use the optometrist to fill that prescription. Most of the opticians' business therefore came from patients who had gotten prescriptions from a medical doctor specializing in eye care (opthalmologist), and from providing, without prescription, duplicate eyeglasses, replacement lenses, and new frames. The opticians feared that the Oklahoma statute, by prohibiting the latter transactions, would deprive the opticians of a substantial portion of their total business. See Brief for Respondents–Appellants Lee Optical of Oklahoma, Inc., at 17–18, 21–22. To whom would that business go? The optometrists.

Lee Optical argued that "optometrists in Oklahoma and elsewhere are in direct competition with opticians in the sale of eyeglasses, frames, and lenses." *Id.* at 20. The Guild of Prescription Opticians and other *amici* also argued that "[t]he inevitable thrust of the statute is optometric monopoly of both refracting and dispensing [eyeglasses]." Brief Amici Curiae of The Guild of Prescription Opticians of America, Inc., et. al., at 384.

Question: Optometrists obviously gained at the expense of opticians under the Oklahoma statute. Who else might have been harmed?

2. The Oklahoma legislature did not happen to pass a statute benefiting optometrists by coincidence. The Oklahoma Optometric Association was involved deeply in having the legislation introduced and steering its passage through the legislature. In its appellate brief, Lee Optical complained about the district court's decision to exclude from evidence a letter dated March 13, 1953 that the Oklahoma Optometric Association had sent to its membership. The letter said the optometrists were "off to war" and that the "spreading menace of the dispensing opticians has forced us to introduce" the challenged bill into the Oklahoma legislature. The letter concluded that "we do not want the dispensing opticians licensed to practice." Brief for Respondents–Appellants Lee Optical of Oklahoma, Inc., at 206.

At the national level, the American Optometric Association had displayed a similar initiative in restricting competition. At the 1954 Annual Congress, the Association adopted a Resolution to recommend "to its affiliated state associations the desirability of causing the introduction of legislation to prevent the indiscriminate sale of ready-made eyeglasses as merchandise so that the unsuspecting and unknowing public may be protected against the dangers which may flow through the use of these articles." Brief in Support of Motion of Pennsylvania Optical Company to file a Brief *Amicus Curiae,* at 4 n.1.

The opportunity under majority rule to profit from legislation that simply reallocates wealth inevitably creates incentives for individuals and groups to attempt just that. Economists use the phrase *rent-seeking* to refer to special interest groups' efforts to promote legislation that redistributes wealth in their favor.

Question: Consider a typical interest group such as the American Petroleum Institute (API), which represents petroleum producers, refiners, and distributors. For what sorts of rent-seeking legislation might the API lobby?

3. From an economic perspective, a pure wealth transfer is a neutral transaction. If society takes $100 from one individual and gives it to another, the loser is poorer and the gainer is richer, but society's overall level of wealth remains unchanged, absent transaction costs. The Oklahoma statute challenged in *Lee Optical* might have involved a pure wealth transfer. If the gains enjoyed by optometrists plus the public benefits of the statute equalled the losses imposed on optometrists and consumers and there were no transaction costs involved, the optometrists' rent-seeking behavior would be neutral from a social welfare perspective.

Questions: Did the special interest legislation passed by the Oklahoma legislature at the optometrists' behest result in a neutral wealth transfer? When might special-interest legislation increase society's wealth? Decrease wealth?

4. Even when rent-seeking legislation results in a pure wealth transfer, the practice may ultimately be destructive of wealth. To understand why, consider the steps a group of optometrists would have to take to

secure protective legislation excluding opticians from making replacement glasses. First, the optometrists must meet and organize for group action. Next a lobbying group like the Oklahoma Optometric Association must be formed, staffed, and given office space and supplies. Then the lobbyists must begin to lobby—drafting proposed legislation, wining and dining State representatives to persuade them to introduce and pass it, perhaps running a media campaign extolling the virtues of the legislation. At the same time, the opticians may be pursuing similar measures.

The opportunity to profit from rent-seeking legislation invites interest groups to compete fiercely to get it. Optometrists and opticians fight over regulation of their respective professions; unions face off against employers on mandatory employment benefits; domestic and foreign auto producers wrestle over import quotas and tariffs; defense contractors squabble over contracts to build nuclear warheads; and the Fraternal Order of Police and the National Rifle Association battle over handgun legislation. But because securing wealth-transferring legislation is a zero-sum game, the costs of competing for such legislation are a deadweight loss to society, a waste. The more competition, the greater the waste. Rent-seeking by special interest groups thus may decrease society's overall wealth and well-being. Moreover, some economists argue that in an efficient rent-seeking market, the superior gains offered by favorable legislation will be competed away until the costs of effective lobbying begin to approach the gains expected from it.

Mancur Olson has argued that in wealthier societies, efforts to redistribute wealth under majority rule grow to overshadow and replace efforts to increase productivity. See M. Olson, The Rise and Decline of Nations (1982).

Question: Does the rule of unanimity pose similar risks of wealth-decreasing rent-seeking behavior?

5. The discussion following Pollock v. Farmer's Loan & Trust Co., above, examined how majority rule invites majority attempts to profit by taking wealth from the minority. *Lee Optical* illustrates how, in a representative democracy peopled by rationally ignorant and apathetic voters and special interest groups willing to lobby and make campaign contributions, it is also possible for the minority to profit by taking wealth from the majority. To determine what sorts of groups are most likely to be successful in securing legislation that redistributes wealth in their favor, consider two of the groups with interests at stake in *Lee Optical:* the optometrists who sold replacement eyewear and the nearsighted consumers who purchased it.

Rational maximizers decide to form an interest group just as they make any other decision, by comparing the costs with the benefits. The benefit of joining an interest group is the individual's expected increase in utility if joining allows the group to lobby successfully for favorable legislation. Thus, the more intense the interest of individual group members, the more likely a group will be formed. Certainly optometrists have a greater stake in excluding opticians from competition than the average nearsighted consumer has in more competitive prices for the occasional pair of replacement glasses she must purchase.

The costs of interest group lobbying include the administrative costs of forming the group as well as the lobbying costs themselves. The Oklahoma Optometric Association was a pre-existing organization originally intended to serve a variety of optometrists' needs in addition to lobbying. Thus, the marginal cost of using the group for lobbying was relatively small. In contrast, the start-up cost of organizing nearsighted Oklahomans into a lobbying group would be very large. Groups already formed to achieve another joint purpose (like labor unions formed to bargain with management or professional organizations such as the ABA) have a distinct cost advantage when it comes to lobbying.

Finally, because a single lobbyist's office can represent ten individuals or ten thousand, it would appear that the individual cost of lobbying is reduced (and lobbying made more attractive) when lobbying costs can be spread among a group with a large membership, rather than a group with a small membership. But such an analysis ignores the freerider effects so often inherent in group action. Successful lobbying is a public good; all optometrists benefitted from the Oklahoma statute, whether they were members of the Oklahoma Optometric Association or not. Mancur Olson argued that because smaller groups can control freeriding more readily, small groups have a lobbying advantage over large ones, and both types have incentive to try to find a way to prevent freeriding. M. Olson, The Logic of Collective Action 11, 21 (1965). A union, for example, might bargain for a "closed shop" contract with management.

The problem of freeriding leads to a phenomenon Olson referred to as "the exploitation of the great by the small." When two individuals are both interested in certain legislation but one has a much greater financial interest than the other, the individual with the lesser interest is likely to sit back and freeride on the efforts of the person with a large amount at stake. Thus, the largest producers in an industry have the greatest incentive to lobby for legislation favorable to the industry while smaller producers are tempted to coast on their efforts. In lobbying against pollution controls or fuel economy standards, General Motors works while Chrysler smirks.

Questions: What other factors might affect a group's success in lobbying for special interest legislation? In particular, how does the relative wealth of groups affect their power in gaining favorable legislation?

6. When groups spend time and money lobbying for particular legislation, they in effect are trying to "buy" a favorable law. According to the economic theory of legislation, Landes & Posner, The Independent Judiciary in an Interest–Group Perspective, 18 J. L. & Econ. 875, 877 (1975):

> Legislation is supplied to groups or coalitions that outbid rival seekers of favorable legislation. The price that the winning group bids is determined by both the value of the legislative protection to the group's members and the group's ability to overcome the free-rider problems that plague coalitions. Payments take the form of campaign contributions, votes, implicit promises of future favors, and sometimes outright bribes. In short, legislation is "sold" by the legislature and "bought" by the beneficiaries of the legislation.

Questions: Assuming that the groups that lobby the hardest are the most likely to succeed, laws, like other market goods, will be channelled to those willing and able to pay the most for them. Isn't that wealth maximizing?

7. The Framers of the U.S. Constitution recognized the temptation for individuals under majority rule to devote scarce resources to the negative-sum game of redistributing wealth. In the Federalist No. 10, Madison argued that individuals are inevitably tempted to be "united and actuated by some common impulse or passion, or of interest, adverse to the rights of other citizens, or to the permanent and aggregate interests of the community," so that "[t]he latent causes of faction are thus sown in the nature of man."

This book's final section examines how one might go about the task faced by the Framers—crafting a Constitution to ensure that government improves, rather than decreases, society's overall level of well-being. As an introduction to that section, consider the Due Process Clauses of the Fifth and Fourteenth Amendments, which provide that neither the federal government nor the states may deprive any person "of life, liberty, or property, without due process of law."

In the early part of this century, the Supreme Court declared that due process required that legislative action bear a "real and substantial relationship" to the public welfare. Under that standard the Court inquired into the merits of legislation and struck down statutes the Justices felt to be unwise, unreasonable, or insufficiently connected to the public interest. See Lochner v. New York, 198 U.S. 45, 25 S.Ct. 539, 49 L.Ed. 937 (1905) (striking down law limiting hours that bakery employees could work during week); Coppage v. Kansas, 236 U.S. 1, 35 S.Ct. 240, 59 L.Ed. 441 (1915) (striking down statute prohibiting employers from requiring employee to agree they would not join unions); Adkins v. Children's Hospital, 261 U.S. 525, 43 S.Ct. 394, 67 L.Ed. 785 (1923) (striking down minimum wage law).

The *Lochner* era of "substantive due process" might be thought of as a judicial attempt to use the Due Process Clauses to check legislative action furthering private redistributive interests more than the public welfare. By the mid-century, however, the Supreme Court had backed away from the *Lochner* philosophy and showed increasing reluctance to second-guess the wisdom of legislative action. Recall Justice Douglas' announcement in *Lee Optical* that "[t]he day is gone when this Court uses the Due Process Clause of the Fourteenth Amendment to strike down state laws, regulatory of business and industrial conditions, because they may be unwise, improvident, or out of harmony with a particular school of thought." The modern Court will uphold state action that does not burden a fundamental right against a Due Process challenge so long as the government's action meets the minimal requirement of being "rationally related" to a "legitimate" government purpose.

Question: Can the rational relation standard effectively deter the use of the legislative process for redistributive ends? Consider Justice Douglas' opinion in *Lee Optical.*

D. CHOOSING OPTIMAL RULES OF DECISION: THE CRAFTING OF A CONSTITUTION

Previous sections of this book explored the relative advantages and disadvantages of unanimity and less-than-unanimity voting rules. Under a rule of unanimity, group action will always improve group welfare because it is always to the advantage of each group member. Otherwise, there would be no unanimous consent. Unfortunately, reaching unanimous agreement can be difficult, not only because of the need for argument and discussion but also because of individuals' incentives to engage in strategic hold-out behavior.

Majority rule reduces opportunities for strategic behavior and allows more decisions to be reached more quickly. However, majority rule carries its own risks. Arrow's Theorem demonstrates that decisions reached under majority voting may not accurately reflect social preferences. Projects approved by a majority may reduce group welfare when dissenters' losses are taken into account. A related problem is the opportunity that majority rule creates for one group to benefit by taking wealth from another. Rational maximizers will exploit the redistributive opportunities of majority rule even when the deadweight losses of redistribution reduce society's overall wealth or utility.

Recognizing that different decisionmaking rules pose different risks leads naturally to the question of constitutions. How can rational individuals entering a social contract tailor decisionmaking rules to maximize social welfare while protecting themselves from harmful redistributive government coercion?

1. EXTERNAL COSTS, DECISIONMAKING COSTS, AND THE ECONOMIC ARGUMENT FOR A CONSTITUTION

J. BUCHANAN & G. TULLOCK, THE CALCULUS OF CONSENT *

(1965)

* * * The possible benefits from collective action may be measured or quantified in terms of reductions in the costs that the private behavior of other individuals is expected to impose on the individual decision-maker [externalities]. However, collective action, if undertaken, will also require that the individual spend some time and effort in making decisions for the group, in reaching agreement with his fellows. More importantly, under certain decision-making rules, choices contrary to the individual's own interest may be made for the group. In any case, participation in collective activity is costly to the individual, and the rational man will take this fact into account at the stage of constitutional choice.

* * * [W]e may develop two cost functions or relationships that will prove helpful. In the first, which we shall call the *external-costs* function, we may relate, for the single individual with respect to a single activity, the costs that he expects to endure as a result of the actions of others to the number of individuals who are required to agree before a final political decision is taken for the group. * * * It is clear that, over the range of decision-making rules, this will normally be a decreasing function: that is to say, as the number of individuals required to agree increases, the expected costs will decrease. When unanimous agreement is dictated by the decision-making rule, the expected costs on the individual must be zero since he will not willingly allow others to impose external costs on him when he can effectively prevent this from happening.

This function is represented geometrically in Figure 1. * * *

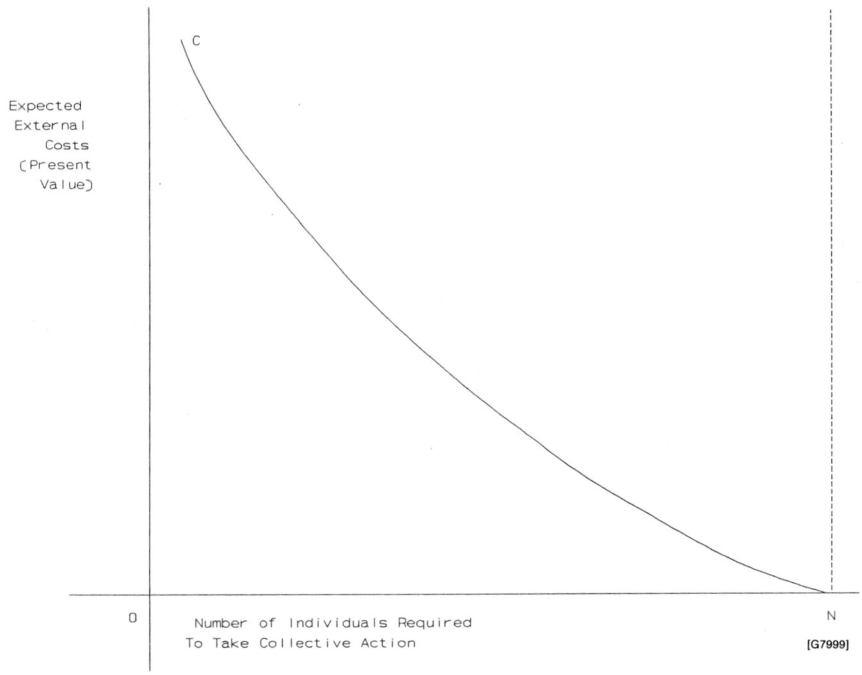

FIGURE 1

* * * Suppose that the decision-making rule is such that a collective action can be taken at any time that any one member of the group dictates it. The single individual can then authorize action for the State, or in the name of the State, which adversely affects others in the group. It seems evident that under such a rule the individual must anticipate that many actions taken by others which are unfavorable to him will take place, and the costs of these actions will be *external costs* in the same sense that the costs expected from private activity might be external. The fact that collective action, under most decision-making rules, involves external costs of this nature has not been adequately

recognized. The private operation of the neighborhood plant with the smoking chimney may impose external costs on the individual by soiling his laundry, but this cost is no more external to the individual's own private calculus than the tax cost imposed on him unwillingly in order to finance the provision of public services to his fellow citizen in another area. Under the extreme decision-making rule which allows any individual in the whole group to order collective action, the expected external costs will be much greater * * *.

* * * We shall employ a simple illustration. Assume that all local public services are financed from property-tax revenues and that the tax rate is automatically adjusted so as to cover all public expenditures. Now assume further that any individual in the municipal group under consideration may secure road or street repairs or improvements when he requests it from city authorities. It is evident that the individual, when he makes a decision, will not take the full marginal costs of the action into account. He will make his decision on the basis of a comparison of his individual marginal costs, a part of total marginal costs only, with individual marginal benefits, which may be equal to total marginal benefits. The individual in this example will be able to secure external benefits by ordering his own street repaired or improved. Since each individual will be led to do this, and since individual benefits will exceed individual costs over a wide extension of the activity there will surely be an over investment in streets and roads, relative to other public and private investments of resources. The rational individual will expect that the general operation of such a decision-making rule will result in positive external costs being imposed on him.

* * *

As we move to the right from point C in Figure 1, the net external costs expected by the individual will tend to fall. If two persons in the group, *any* two, are required to reach agreement before collective action is authorized, there will be fewer decisions that the individual expects to run contrary to his own desires. In a similar fashion, we may proceed over the more and more inclusive decision-making rules. If the agreement of three persons is required, the individual will expect lower external costs than under the two-person rule, etc. * * * So long as there remains any possibility that the individual will be affected adversely by a collective decision, expected net external costs will be positive. These costs vanish only with the rule of unanimity. * * *

* * *

If collective action is to be taken, someone must participate in the decision-making. Recognizing this, we may derive, in very general terms, a second cost relationship or function. * * * If two or more persons are required to agree on a *single* decision, time and effort of another sort is introduced—that which is required to secure agreement. Moreover, these costs will increase as the size of the group required to agree increases. As a collective decision-making rule is changed to include a larger and larger proportion of the total group, these costs may increase at an increasing rate. As unanimity is approached, dramatic increases in expected decision-making costs may be predicted. In fact, when unanimity is approached, the situation becomes radically different from that existing through the range of less inclusive rules. * * * Individual investment in strategic bargaining becomes highly rational, and the costs imposed by such bargaining are likely to be high.

* * * [T]he rewards received by voters in any such agreement would be directly proportionate to their stubbornness and apparent unreasonableness during the bargaining stage. If we include (as we should) the opportunity costs of bargains that are never made, it seems likely that the bargaining costs might approach infinity in groups of substantial size. * * * Thus our bargaining-cost function operates in two ranges: in the lower reaches it represents mainly the problems of making up an agreed bargain among a group of people, any one of whom can readily be replaced. Here, as a consequence, there is little incentive to invest resources in strategic bargaining. Near unanimity, investments in strategic bargaining are apt to be great, and the expected costs very high.

* * * Figure 2 illustrates the relationship geometrically.

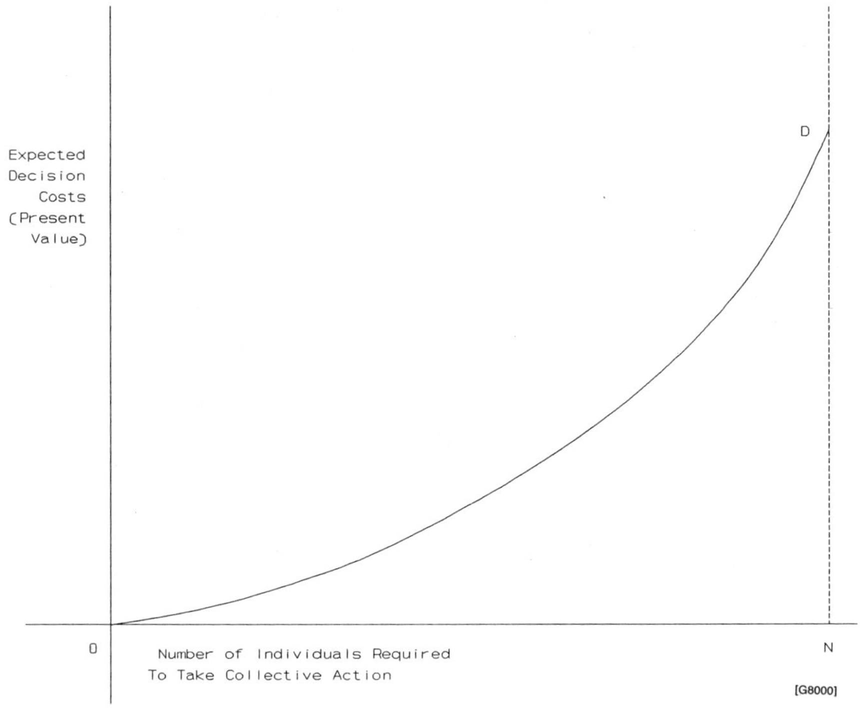

FIGURE 2

* * * For a given activity the fully rational individual, at the time of constitutional choice, will try to choose that decision-making rule which will *minimize* the present value of the expected costs that he

must suffer. He will do so by minimizing the *sum* of the expected external costs and expected decision-making costs, as we have defined these separate components. Geometrically, we add the two costs functions vertically. The "optimal" or most "efficient" decision-making rule, *for the individual whose expectations are depicted and for the activity or set of activities that he is considering,* will be that shown by the lowest point on the resulting curve. Figure 3 is illustrative: the individual will choose the rule which requires that K/N of the group agree when collective decisions are made.

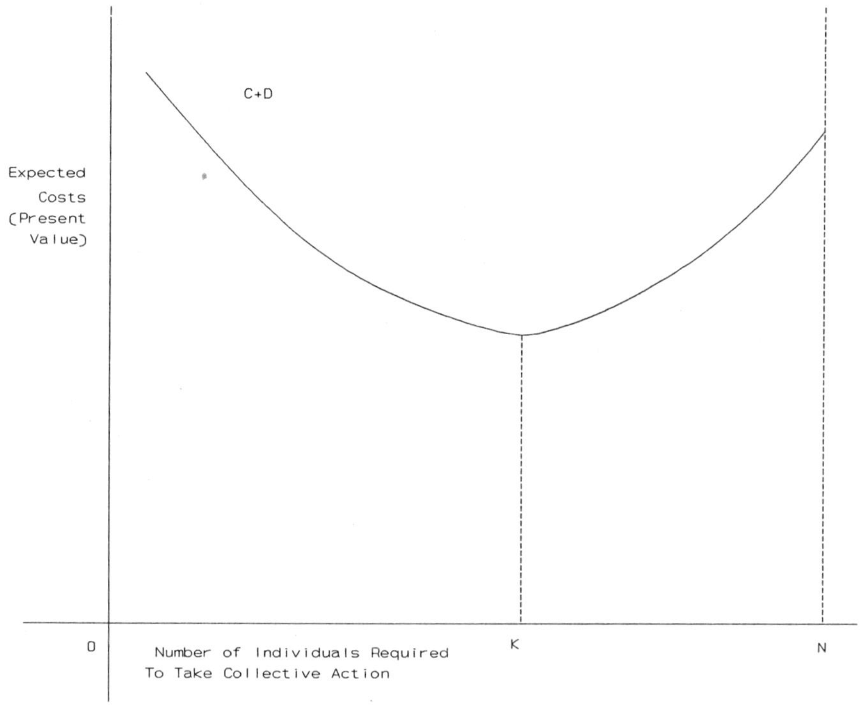

FIGURE 3

[G8001]

* * *

* * * The rational individual, at the stage of constitutional choice, confronts a calculus not unlike that which he must face in making his everyday economic choices. By agreeing to more inclusive rules, he is accepting the additional burden to decision-making in exchange for additional protection against adverse decisions. In moving in the opposing direction toward a less inclusive decision-making rule, the individual is trading some of his protection against external costs for a lowered cost of decision-making.

* * *

What are some of the implications of the analysis of individual choice of constitutional rules that has been developed? First of all, that analysis suggests that it is rational to *have a constitution.* By this is meant that it will be rational for the individual to choose more than one decision-making rule for collective choice-making under normal circumstances. If a single rule is to be chosen for all collective decision, no constitution in the normal sense will exist.

The second, and most significant, implication of our analysis is that at no point in the discussion has it seemed useful or appropriate to introduce the *one* particular decision-making rule that has traditionally been very closely associated with theories of democracy. We have not found occasion to refer specifically to the rule of majority decision, or, in more definite terms, to the rule described by $(N/2 + 1)/N$. The analysis has shown that the rule of unanimity does possess certain special attributes, since it is only through the adoption of this rule that the individual can insure himself against the external damage that may be caused by the actions of other individuals, privately or collectively. However, in our preliminary analysis, once the rule of unanimity is departed from, there seems to be nothing to distinguish sharply any one rule from any other.

Notes and Questions

1. A person in the state of nature, without government, can freely impose his external costs on others but also must suffer the externalities others impose on him. Social theorists from Hobbes to Rawls have assumed that the likely result is a world where society's overall level of well-being falls well below the level possible when a coercive state keeps order and controls externalities.

Buchanan and Tullock point out that a state also imposes at least two kinds of costs. One is the "external cost" of state coercion itself. Citizens suffer costs whenever the government forces them to do something they would rather not do: pay taxes, refrain from stealing from their neighbors' property, serve in the military. A second cost of state action is the "decisionmaking cost" of meeting, discussing, and voting over what state action is appropriate. The expected external costs of government coercion decrease as the proportion of group support required to take state action increases; when unanimous consent is required, no one suffers coercion. But the decisionmaking costs of government action increase as decisionmaking rules become more inclusive. Decisions by a single individual are easy to make. Unanimous group decisions are sometimes impossible.

The rational individual calculating the costs of government intervention will take account of both types of costs. Rational maximizers will choose the decisionmaking rule that permits action to be taken at least cost, including decisionmaking costs and potential external costs from state coercion.

2. The rule of unanimity is qualitatively different from any non-unanimous rule because only the former eliminates all risk of external costs from government coercion. Buchanan and Tullock suggest that once unanimity is abandoned, rules allowing group action on less-than-unanimous agreement differ only quantitatively, in the degree of decisionmaking and external costs they impose. In particular, there is nothing special about "traditional" majority rule (greater than 50% approval). One might just as well require 30%, 40%, or 60% approval.

There may, however, be some advantage to requiring at least 50%-plus approval for group action. Suppose a group adopts a decisionmaking rule requiring the support of 40% of group members to authorize group action. Approximately 55% of the group support daylight savings time; 45% want to abolish it.

Questions: Will a motion to abolish daylight savings pass? Will a subsequent motion to reverse that decision pass? What are the advantages of requiring 50%-plus approval?

3. The U. S. Constitution provides for a representative government rather than a true democracy where all citizens vote on all issues.

Question: How does representative government reflect the decisionmaking costs associated with group action?

4. Within the context of a representative system, the Constitution provides different decisionmaking rules for different social decisions. Citizens elect members of Congress by plurality vote. Once elected, the legislators use traditional majority rule and statutes are passed only if supported by more than half the members of both House and Senate. It takes a two-thirds vote of both Houses to override a Presidential veto, and a two-thirds vote of both Houses followed by three-quarters state ratification to amend the Constitution.

Question: Buchanan and Tullock suggest a less-inclusive decisionmaking rule is appropriate when decisionmaking costs are high and/or the risk of inefficient external costs from government action is low, and a more inclusive rule is appropriate when the reverse is true. Is the pattern of decisionmaking rules presented in the U.S. Constitution consistent with their analysis?

5. Buchanan and Tullock approach choosing optimal decisionmaking rules from a single individual's perspective. But different state actions pose different risks for different individuals. Persons with high incomes may be particularly sensitive to the potential external costs of a progressive income tax; farmers may be concerned about decisions to eliminate agricultural subsidies; workers and employers each may worry (for different reasons) about minimum wage laws. Thus, different individuals may demand more-inclusive decisionmaking rules for different issues. The problem for constitutional formation is molding such differing preferences into a single recipe for group action.

The now-familiar solution is to place individuals at the constitutional stage in an "original position" where they do not know which forms of government intervention pose the greatest risk to their particular interests. All individuals choose decisionmaking rules from the same perspective—that of the "average" member of the society-to-be. That average individual will choose the decisionmaking rule that imposes the lowest decisionmaking and external costs, on average, for a particular type of issue.

Buchanan's and Tullock's solution in The Calculus of Consent 77–78 resembles Rawls':

> Agreement seems more likely on general rules for collective choice than on the later choices to be made *within* the confines of certain agreed-upon rules. * * * Essential to the analysis is the presumption

that the individual is *uncertain* as to what his own precise role will be in any one of the whole chain of later collective choices that will actually have to be made. * * * [T]he individual will not find it advantageous to vote for rules that may promote sectional, class, or group interests because, by presupposition, he is unable to predict the role that he will be playing in the actual collective decision-making process at any particular time in the future. He cannot predict with any degree of certainty whether he is more likely to be in a winning or a losing coalition on any specific issue.

Question: Buchanan and Tullock assert that "[t]he uncertainty that is required in order for the individual to be led by his own interest to support constitutional provisions that are generally advantageous to all individuals and to all groups seems likely to be present at any constitutional state of discussion." *Id.* Is that a valid assumption?

Varying the degree of inclusiveness of voting rules is just one of many potential devices rational individuals drafting a constitution might use to encourage a coercive state to serve the public welfare rather than to engage in wealth-destroying redistributive schemes. The remainder of this book examines other constitutional doctrines that may channel state action towards welfare maximization and away from intervention and rent-seeking that makes society worse off.

2. EFFICIENT STATE INTERVENTION

DeSHANEY v. WINNEBAGO COUNTY DEPARTMENT OF SOCIAL SERVICES

Supreme Court of the United States, 1989.
489 U.S. 189, 109 S.Ct. 998, 103 L.Ed.2d 249.

REHNQUIST, CHIEF JUSTICE.

Petitioner is a boy who was beaten and permanently injured by his father, with whom he lived. Respondents are social workers and other local officials who received complaints that petitioner was being abused by his father and had reason to believe that this was the case, but nonetheless did not act to remove petitioner from his father's custody. Petitioner sued respondents claiming that their failure to act deprived him of his liberty in violation of the Due Process Clause of the Fourteenth Amendment to the United States Constitution. We hold that it did not.

* * *

The Due Process Clause of the Fourteenth Amendment provides that "[n]o State shall ... deprive any person of life, liberty, or property, without due process of law." Petitioners contend that the State deprived Joshua of his liberty interest in "free[dom] from ... unjustified intrusions on personal security," by failing to provide him with adequate protection against his father's violence. * * *

But nothing in the language of the Due Process Clause itself requires the State to protect the life, liberty, and property of its citizens against invasion by private actors. The Clause is phrased as a limitation on the State's power to act, not as a guarantee of certain minimal levels of safety and security. It forbids the State itself to deprive individuals of life, liberty, or property without "due process of law," but its language cannot fairly be extended to impose an affirmative obligation on the State to ensure that those interests do not come to harm through other means. * * * Its purpose was to protect the people from the State, not to ensure that the State protected them from each other. The Framers were content to leave the extent of governmental obligation in the latter area to the democratic political processes.

* * *

* * * Petitioners concede that the harms Joshua suffered did not occur while he was in the State's custody, but while he was in the custody of his natural father, who was in no sense a state actor. While the State may have been aware of the dangers that Joshua faced in the free world, it played no part in their creation, nor did it do anything to render him any more vulnerable to them. * * * Under these circumstances, the State had no constitutional duty to protect Joshua.

* * *

Judges and lawyers, like other humans, are moved by natural sympathy in a case like this to find a way for Joshua and his mother to receive adequate compensation for the grievous harm inflicted upon them. But before yielding to that impulse, it is well to remember once again that the harm was inflicted not by the State of Wisconsin, but by Joshua's father. The most that can be said of the state functionaries in this case is that they stood by and did nothing when suspicious circumstances dictated a more active role for them. In defense of them it must also be said that had they moved too soon to take custody of the son away from the father, they would likely have met with charges of improperly intruding into the parent-child relationship * * *.

The people of Wisconsin may well prefer a system of liability which would place upon the State and its officials the responsibility for failure to act in situations such as the present one. They may create such a system, if they do not have it already, by changing the tort law of the State in accordance with the regular lawmaking process. But they should not have it thrust upon them by this Court's expansion of the Due Process Clause of the Fourteenth Amendment.

AFFIRMED.

Notes and Questions

1. Uncontrolled individuals in the state of nature often either engage in activities that impose external costs on others or decline to act in a

fashion that would confer external benefits. Social contract theory suggests that the principal function of a coercive state is to regulate individual behavior in order to minimize costs and maximize benefits.

It was undoubtably welfare-reducing as well as cruel for the State of Wisconsin to allow Joshua's father to beat him until "he suffered brain damage so severe that he is expected to spend the rest of his life confined to an institution for the profoundly retarded." 489 U.S. at 193, 109 S.Ct. at 1002. Although Mr. DeShaney presumably derived some utility from beating his son, his pleasure probably was far outweighed by the pain of Joshua's severe and permanent injury. The State could have prevented the tremendous pecuniary and nonpecuniary costs arising from Joshua's injury if it had taken a more active role in supervising Mr. DeShaney's childrearing practices and intervened when it appeared Joshua might be harmed.

Nevertheless, there is no Constitutional requirement that the State of Wisconsin protect Joshua from his father. Nor, as Justice Rehnquist's opinion notes, did the Wisconsin voters feel it worthwhile to pass a statute requiring more active State supervision of childrearing and custody decisions. Wisely or unwisely, the vast majority of children in Wisconsin and elsewhere are raised with little or no state intervention.

> *Questions:* Are there economic reasons why the state should decline to monitor parents closely in order to prevent harmful childrearing practices? Recalling Buchanan's and Tullock's discussion of the costs of group action, what costs would have been incurred preventing Joshua's injury? More generally, why might rational maximizers drafting a social contract balk at requiring the state to eliminate all external harms?

2. Individuals suffering from external harms have a third option other than simply enduring the harm or submitting to coercive government intervention. That option is to reduce or eliminate the inefficiency through *voluntary* arrangements. One area where capitalist societies tend to rely on voluntary arrangements instead of government directives to allocate resources efficiently is the commercial market for goods and services. Individuals can channel resources to higher-valued uses through exchange without need for government intervention.

> *Question:* Goods and services can be allocated by government directive rather than through a free market. Indeed, many of the formerly communist governments allocated by directive. Why might it be advantageous to rely on voluntary arrangements instead?

3. The potential for private voluntary arrangements to reduce externalities extends far beyond the simple case of an exchange between two individuals. Homeowner's associations and recreational clubs are other examples of voluntary arrangements designed to increase group well-being by overcoming externalities.

Buchanan and Tullock suggest that the costs of government intervention include decisionmaking costs plus the external costs that government coercion imposes on the coerced individuals.

Question: How do the costs of correcting externalities through voluntary arrangements resemble, and differ from, the costs of state intervention?

4. Individuals faced with external harms in the state of nature have three options: do nothing and suffer the costs others impose, as in Hobbes' state of nature (SON); undertake voluntary action which reduces those external costs but imposes its own transactions costs (V); and employ a government authority that reduces or eliminates the external costs that others impose but imposes its own operating costs and the risk of external costs from state coercion (G). Rational individuals will choose the option—SON, V, or G—that minimizes the *sum* of those varying costs. Sometimes it is cheapest to do nothing; sometimes state regulation is best; and sometimes costs are best minimized through voluntary transactions.

Question: Consider the following activities involving external costs or benefits: choosing a car color, allocating consumer goods, and arranging police protection and a national defense. Which option—SON, V, or G—is the most appropriate response to the externalities associated with those activities?

3. THE INDEPENDENT JUDICIARY

MARBURY v. MADISON

Supreme Court of the United States, 1803.
5 U.S. (1 Cranch) 137, 2 L.Ed. 60.

MARSHALL, CHIEF JUSTICE.

* * * [A] rule was granted in this case, requiring the secretary of state to show cause why a mandamus should not issue, directing him to deliver to William Marbury his commission as a justice of the peace for the county of Washington, in the District of Columbia.

* * *

Mr. Marbury * * * was appointed; * * * the appointment was not revocable, but vested in the officer legal rights, which are protected by the laws of his country.

* * *

The government of the United States has been emphatically termed a government of laws, and not of men. It will certainly cease to deserve this high appellation, if the laws furnish no remedy for the violation of a vested legal right.

* * *

This, then, is a plain case for a mandamus, either to deliver the commission, or a copy of it from the record: and it only remains to be inquired,

Whether it can issue from this court.

The act to establish the judicial courts of the United States authorizes the Supreme Court "to issue writs of mandamus in cases warranted by the principles and usages of law, to any courts appointed, or persons holding office, under the authority of the United States."

The Secretary of State, being a person holding an office under the authority of the United States, is precisely within the letter of the description, and if this court is not authorized to issue a writ of mandamus to such an officer, it must be because the law is unconstitutional, and therefore absolutely incapable of conferring the authority, and assigning the duties which its words purport to confer and assign.

The constitution vests the whole judicial power of the United States in one Supreme Court, and such inferior courts as congress shall, from time to time, ordain and establish. * * *

In the distribution of this power it is declared that "the Supreme Court shall have original jurisdiction in all cases affecting ambassadors, other public ministers and consuls, and those in which a state shall be a party. In all other cases, the Supreme Court shall have appellate jurisdiction."

* * *

To enable this court, then, to issue a mandamus, it must be shown to be an exercise of appellate jurisdiction * * *.

* * *

It is the essential criterion of appellate jurisdiction, that it revises and corrects the proceedings in a cause already instituted, and does not create that cause. * * * [T]o issue such a writ [of mandamus] to an officer for the delivery of a paper, is in effect the same as to sustain an original action for that paper, and, therefore, seems not to belong to appellate, but to original jurisdiction. * * *

The authority, therefore, given to the Supreme Court, by the act establishing the judicial courts of the United States, to issue writs of mandamus to public officers, appears not to be warranted by the constitution; and it becomes necessary to inquire whether a jurisdiction so conferred can be exercised.

The question, whether an act, repugnant to the constitution, can become the law of the land, is a question deeply interesting to the United States; but, happily, not of an intricacy proportioned to its interest. It seems only necessary to recognize certain principles, supposed to have been long and well established, to decide it.

That the people have an original right to establish, for their future government, such principles, as, in their opinion, shall most conduce to their own happiness is the basis on which the whole American fabric has been erected. * * *

* * *

Certainly all those who have framed written constitutions contemplate them as forming the fundamental and paramount law of the nation, and, consequently, the theory of every such government must be, that an act of the legislature, repugnant to the constitution, is void.

* * *

If an act of the legislature, repugnant to the constitution, is void, does it, notwithstanding its invalidity, bind the courts, and oblige them to give it effect? * * *

It is emphatically the province and duty of the judicial department to say what the law is. Those who apply the rule to particular cases, must of necessity expound and interpret that rule. If two laws conflict with each other, the courts must decide on the operation of each.

So if a law be in the opposition to the constitution; if both the law and the constitution apply to a particular case, so that the court must either decide that case conformably to the law, disregarding the constitution; or conformably to the constitution, disregarding the law; the court must determine which of these conflicting rules governs the case. This is of the very essence of judicial duty.

If, then, the courts are to regard the constitution, and the constitution is superior to any ordinary act of the legislature, the constitution, and not such ordinary act, must govern the case to which they both apply.

* * *

* * * [I]t is apparent, that the framers of the constitution contemplated that instrument as a rule for the government of courts, as well as of the legislature.

Why otherwise does it direct the judges to take an oath to support it? * * *

It is also not entirely unworthy of observation, that in declaring what shall be the supreme law of the land, the constitution itself is first mentioned; and not the laws of the United States generally * * *.

Thus, the particular phraseology of the constitution of the United States confirms and strengthens the principle, supposed to be essential to all written constitutions, and that a law repugnant to the constitution is void; and that courts, as well as other departments, are bound by that instrument.

The rule must be discharged.

Notes and Questions

1. *Marbury* held that legislation that conflicts with the U.S. Constitution is void and unenforceable, and that it is the court's role rather than the legislature's to "say what the law is" and determine when constitution and statute conflict.

Questions: Why might rational maximizers drafting a constitution want to ensure that the constitution's provisions trump inconsistent legislation subsequently passed under majority rule? Why might they create an independent government branch to determine when legislation conflicts with constitutional provisions rather than leave the question of constitutionality to the legislature?

2. The economic theory of legislation supposes that statutes are the product of interest group lobbying in the legislature. A court that strikes down legislation on constitutional grounds would appear to interfere with that process and to curb legislative catering to special interests.

In The Independent Judiciary: An Interest–Group Perspective, 18 J. L. & Econ. 875, 879 (1975), William Landes and Richard Posner argued that rather than interfering with competition for legislation, an independent judiciary actually benefits interest groups hoping to extract favorable laws. They note that the economic theory of legislation portrays statutes as "bargains" between legislators and interest groups who lobby legislators and promise them political support. Unlike private contracts, however, bargains between politicians and interest groups are not binding.

> Legislation is not self-enforcing, however. If the people subject to a law refuse to obey it, recourse to the courts is necessary to enforce the law. A judiciary that was subservient to the current membership of the legislature could nullify legislation enacted in a previous session of the legislature. * * * Insofar as judges are merely agents of the current legislature, they will utilize their considerable interpretive leeway to rewrite the legislation in conformity with the views of the current rather than the enacting legislature and they will thereby impair the "contract" between the enacting legislature and the group that procured this legislation.
>
> If we assume that an independent judiciary would, in contrast, interpret and apply legislation in accordance with the original legislative understanding (an assumption examined shortly) it follows that an independent judiciary facilitates rather than, as conventionally believed, limits the practice of interest-group politics.

Questions: How does an independent judiciary further bargaining between legislators and interest groups by enforcing the terms of the original bargain underlying a statute? Can Landes' and Posner's view of the court's role be reconciled with the notion that the courts are a check on legislative authority? Consider the different roles courts play when they strike down statutes on constitutional grounds, and when they resolve issues of statutory interpretation between parties who disagree on a statute's meaning.

3. Article III of the U.S. Constitution provides that federal judges enjoy life tenure, and that Congress may not reduce judges' salaries while they remain in office.

Questions: How might Article III's provisions help the judiciary better serve the goal of maximizing society's well-being? How might those provisions threaten social welfare?

4. SEPARATION OF POWERS AND BICAMERALISM

IMMIGRATION AND NATURALIZATION SERVICE v. CHADHA

Supreme Court of the United States, 1983.
462 U.S. 919, 103 S.Ct. 2764, 77 L.Ed.2d 317.

BURGER, CHIEF JUSTICE.

* * * [This case] presents a challenge to the constitutionality of the provision in § 244(c)(2) of the Immigration and Nationality Act, authorizing one House of Congress, by resolution, to invalidate the decision of the Executive Branch, pursuant to authority delegated by Congress to the Attorney General of the United States, to allow a particular deportable alien to remain in the United States.

[Chadha was born in Kenya and lawfully admitted to the United States in 1966 on a nonimmigrant student visa. His visa expired in 1972. Pursuant to § 244(c)(1), an immigration judge suspended Chadha's deportation and Attorney General conveyed to Congress a report recommending against deportation. A resolution opposing granting permanent United States residence to six aliens, including Chadha, was introduced in the House of Representatives and passed. Pursuant to § 244(c)(2), the resolution was not submitted to the Senate for a vote, nor to the President for signing. After the House vetoed the Attorney General's decision to allow Chadha to remain in the United States, the immigration judge reopened deportation proceedings. Chadha moved to terminate the proceedings on the ground that the Congress' veto of the Attorney General's decision under § 244(c)(2) was unconstitutional.]

* * *

* * * [T]he fact that a given law or procedure is efficient, convenient, and useful in facilitating functions of government, standing alone, will not save it if it is contrary to the Constitution. Convenience and efficiency are not the primary objectives—or the hallmarks—of democratic government and our inquiry is sharpened rather than blunted by the fact that congressional veto provisions are appearing with increasing frequency in statutes which delegate authority to executive and independent agencies * * *.

* * *

Explicit and unambiguous provisions of the Constitution prescribe and define the respective functions of the Congress and of the Executive in the legislative process. Since the precise terms of those familiar provisions are critical to the resolution of this case, we set them out verbatim. Art. I provides:

> "All legislative Powers herein granted shall be vested in a Congress of the United States, which shall consist of a Senate *and* a House of Representatives." (Emphasis added).

> "Every Bill which shall have passed the House of Representatives *and* the Senate, *shall,* before it becomes a Law, be presented to the President of the United States * * * " (Emphasis added).
>
> "*Every* Order, Resolution, or Vote to which the Concurrence of the Senate and House of Representatives may be necessary (except on a question of Adjournment) *shall* be presented to the President of the United States; and before the Same shall take Effect, *shall* be approved by him, or being disapproved by him, *shall* be repassed by two thirds of the Senate and House of Representatives, according to the Rules and Limitations prescribed in the Case of a Bill." (Emphasis added).

These provisions of Art. I are integral parts of the constitutional design for the separation of powers. * * *

* * *

The President's role in the lawmaking process [reflects] the Framers' careful efforts to check whatever propensity a particular Congress might have to enact oppressive, improvident, or ill-considered measures. The President's veto role in the legislative process was described later during public debate on ratification:

> "It establishes a salutary check upon the legislative body, calculated to guard the community against the effects of faction, precipitancy, or of any impulse unfriendly to the public good which may happen to influence a majority of that body * * *." The Federalist No. 73, *supra,* at 458 (A. Hamilton).

The Court also has observed that the Presentment Clauses serve the important purpose of assuring that a "national" perspective is grafted on the legislative process:

> "The President is a representative of the people just as the members of the Senate and of the House are, and it may be, at some times, on some subjects, that the President elected by all the people is rather more representative of them all than are the members of either body of the Legislature whose constituencies are local and not countrywide * * *."

The bicameral requirement of Art. I, §§ 1, 7 was of scarcely less concern to the Framers than was the Presidential veto and indeed the two concepts are interdependent. * * *

* * *

However familiar, it is useful to recall that apart from their fear that special interests could be favored at the expense of public needs, the Framers were also concerned, although not of one mind, over the apprehensions of the smaller states. Those states feared a commonality of interest among the larger states would work to their disadvantage; representatives of the larger states, on the other hand, were skeptical of a legislature that could pass laws favoring a minority of the people. It need hardly be repeated here that the Great Compromise, under which one House was viewed as representing the people and the other the states, allayed the fears of both the large and small states.

We see therefore that the Framers were acutely conscious that the bicameral requirement and the Presentment Clauses would serve essential constitutional functions. * * * It emerges clearly that the prescription for legislative action in Art. I represents the Framers' decision that the legislative power of the Federal government be exercised in accord with a single, finely wrought and exhaustively considered, procedure.

* * *

* * * After long experience with the clumsy, time-consuming private bill procedure, Congress made a deliberate choice to delegate to the Executive Branch, and specifically to the Attorney General, the authority to allow deportable aliens to remain in this country in certain specified circumstances. It is not disputed that this choice to delegate authority is precisely the kind of decision that can be implemented only in accordance with the procedures set out in Art. I. Disagreement with the Attorney General's decision on Chadha's deportation—that is, Congress' decision to deport Chadha—no less than Congress' original choice to delegate to the Attorney General the authority to make that decision, involves determinations of policy that Congress can implement in only one way; bicameral passage followed by presentment to the President. Congress must abide by its delegation of authority until that delegation is legislatively altered or revoked.

* * *

The veto authorized by § 244(c)(2) doubtless has been in many respects a convenient shortcut; the "sharing" with the Executive by Congress of its authority over aliens in this manner is, on its face, an appealing compromise. In purely practical terms, it is obviously easier for action to be taken by one House without submission to the President; but it is crystal clear from the records of the Convention, contemporaneous writings and debates, that the Framers ranked other values higher than efficiency. * * *

The choices we discern as having been made in the Constitutional Convention impose burdens on governmental processes that often seem clumsy, inefficient, even unworkable, but those hard choices were consciously made by men who had lived under a form of government that permitted arbitrary governmental acts to go unchecked. * * * With all the obvious flaws of delay, untidiness, and potential for abuse, we have not yet found a better way to preserve freedom than by making the exercise of power subject to the carefully crafted restraints spelled out in the Constitution.

We hold that the Congressional veto provision in § 244(c)(2) is severable from the Act and that it is unconstitutional. Accordingly, the judgment of the Court of Appeals is

Affirmed.

Notes and Questions

1. The constitutional requirements that legislation be passed by both Houses and then presented to the President are inconvenient and cumber-

some. In Buchanan's and Tullock's terms, those requirements increase decisionmaking costs. A rational maximizer might still prefer to adopt such a system.

Consider the Presidential veto. Suppose a society decided to make public decisions according to majority rule in a national legislature of nine representatives. Each representative is elected by majority vote from a district with nine voters. The total number of voters in the nation is therefore 81. Consider the effect of adding a president with power to veto legislation, who is elected by a simply majority of all 81 voters.

> *Questions:* What is the smallest number of voters who could push through legislation in the absence of a presidential veto? With a presidential veto? In economic terms, what purpose is served by a veto that increases decisionmaking costs?

2. Article I's bicameral requirement ensures that no federal legislation is passed without the approval of both a majority of the Senate and of the House. Two different classes of representative politicians—House members and Senators—have group power to veto legislation proposed by the other House.

> *Questions:* What interests or constituencies are likely to be served by Senators and Representatives, respectively? What possible advantage might follow from giving those constituencies a veto over proposed legislation?

5. RATIONALITY REVIEW AND THE REQUIREMENT OF PUBLIC PURPOSE

HAWAII HOUSING AUTHORITY v. MIDKIFF

Supreme Court of the United States, 1984.
467 U.S. 229, 104 S.Ct. 2321, 81 L.Ed.2d 186.

O'CONNOR, JUSTICE.

The Fifth Amendment of the United States Constitution provides, in pertinent part, that "private property [shall not] be taken for public use, without just compensation." These cases present the question whether the Public Use Clause of that Amendment, made applicable to the States through the Fourteenth Amendment, prohibits the State of Hawaii from taking, with just compensation, title in real property from lessors and transferring it to lessees in order to reduce the concentration of ownership of fees simple in the State. We conclude that it does not.

The Hawaiian Islands were originally settled by Polynesian immigrants from the western Pacific. These settlers developed an economy around a feudal land tenure system in which one island high chief, the ali'i nui, controlled the land and assigned it for development to certain subchiefs. * * *

Beginning in the early 1800's, Hawaiian leaders and American settlers repeatedly attempted to divide the lands of the kingdom among the crown, the chiefs, and the common people. These efforts proved largely unsuccessful, however, and the land remained in the hands of a few. In the mid–1960's, after extensive hearings, the Hawaii Legislature discovered that while the State and Federal Governments owned almost 49% of the State's land, another 47% was in the hands of only 72 private landowners. * * * The legislature concluded that concentrated land ownership was responsible for skewing the State's residential fee simple market, inflating land prices and injuring the public tranquility and welfare.

To redress these problems, the legislature decided to compel the large landowners to break up their estates. * * * [T]he Hawaii Legislature enacted the Land Reform Act of 1967 (Act), which created a mechanism for condemning residential tracts and for transferring ownership of the condemned fees simple to existing lessees. * * *

* * *

* * * [T]he Court of Appeals [for the Ninth Circuit] determined that the Act could not pass the requisite judicial scrutiny of the Public Use Clause. It found that the transfers contemplated by the Act were unlike those of takings previously held to constitute "public uses" by this Court. The court further determined that the public purposes offered by the Hawaii Legislature were not deserving of judicial deference. The court concluded that the Act was simply "a naked attempt on the part of the state of Hawaii to take the private property of A and transfer it to B solely for B's private use and benefit." * * *

* * *

The starting point for our analysis of the Act's constitutionality is the Court's decision in *Berman v. Parker.* In *Berman,* the Court held constitutional the District of Columbia Redevelopment Act of 1945. That Act provided both for the comprehensive use of the eminent domain power to redevelop slum areas and for the possible sale or lease of the condemned lands to private interests. In discussing whether the takings authorized by that Act were for a "public use," the Court stated:

> "We deal, in other words, with what traditionally has been known as the police power. * * * [W]hen the legislature has spoken, the public interest has been declared in terms well-nigh conclusive. In such cases the legislature, not the judiciary, is the main guardian of the public needs to be served by social legislation * * * This principle admits of no exception merely because the power of eminent domain is involved * * *."

The Court explicitly recognized the breadth of the principle it was announcing, noting:

> "Once the object is within the authority of Congress, the right to realize it through the exercise of eminent domain is clear. For the power of eminent domain is merely the means to the end.... Once the object is within the authority of Congress, the means by which it

> will be attained is also for Congress to determine. Here one of the means chosen is the use of private enterprise for redevelopment of the area. Appellants argue that this makes the project a taking from one businessman for the benefit of another businessman. But the means of executing the project are for Congress and Congress alone to determine, once the public purposes has been established."

The "public use" requirement is thus coterminous with the scope of a sovereign's police powers.

There is a role for courts to play in reviewing a legislature's judgment of what constitutes a public use, even when the eminent domain power is equated with the police power. But the Court in *Berman* made clear that it is "an extremely narrow" one. * * *

To be sure, the Court's cases have repeatedly stated that "one person's property may not be taken for the benefit of another private person without a justifying public purpose, even though compensation be paid." * * * But where the exercise of the eminent domain power is rationally related to a conceivable public purpose, the Court has never held a compensated taking to be proscribed by the Public Use Clause.

On this basis, we have no trouble concluding that the Hawaii Act is constitutional. The people of Hawaii have attempted, much as the settlers of the original 13 Colonies did, to reduce the perceived social and economic evils of a land oligopoly traceable to their monarchs. The land oligopoly has, according to the Hawaii Legislature, created artificial deterrents to the normal functioning of the State's residential land market and forced thousands of individual homeowners to lease, rather than buy, the land underneath their homes. Regulating oligopoly and the evils associated with it is a classic exercise of a State's police powers. We cannot disapprove of Hawaii's exercise of this power.

Nor can we condemn as irrational the Act's approach to correcting the land oligopoly problem. * * *

Of course, this Act, like any other, may not be successful in achieving its intended goals. But "whether *in fact* the provision will accomplish its objectives is not the question: the [constitutional requirement] is satisfied if ... the ... Legislature *rationally could have believed* that the [Act] would promote its objective." When the legislature's purpose is legitimate and its means are not irrational, our cases make clear that empirical debates over the wisdom of takings—no less than debates over the wisdom of other kinds of socioeconomic legislation—are not to be carried out in the federal courts. Redistribution of fees simple to correct deficiencies in the market determined by the state legislature to be attributable to land oligopoly is a rational exercise of the eminent domain power. Therefore, the Hawaii statute must pass the scrutiny of the Public Use Clause.

* * *

The State of Hawaii has never denied that the Constitution forbids even a compensated taking of property when executed for no reason other than to confer a private benefit on a particular private party. A purely private taking could not withstand the scrutiny of the public use requirement; it would serve no legitimate purpose of government and would be void. But no purely private taking is involved in these cases. The Hawaii Legislature enacted its Land Reform Act not to benefit a particular class of identifiable individuals but to attack certain perceived evils of concentrated property ownership in Hawaii—a legitimate public purpose. Use of the condemnation power to achieve this purpose is not irrational. Since we assume for purposes of these appeals that the weighty demand of just compensation has been met, the requirements of the Fifth and Fourteenth Amendments have been satisfied. Accordingly, we reverse the judgment of the Court of Appeals, and remand these cases for further proceedings in conformity with this opinion.

It is so ordered.

Notes and Questions

1. The state may exercise its coercive "police power" to require vaccination (*Jacobson*); to take property (*Midkiff*); and even to imprison innocent individuals (*Korematsu*). Nevertheless, the Constitution circumscribes the state's authority. Among other limitations, state action is confined by a requirement that it serve more than purely private interests.

In *Midkiff,* Justice O'Connor found the requirement of "public use" in the language of the Takings Clause itself. A similar limitation is implied in Supreme Court cases under the Due Process and Equal Protection clauses requiring state actions and classifications to be rationally related to a legitimate "public purpose." See discussion following *Bowers* and *U.N. Declaration of Human Rights,* above.

The requirement that state action be directed to public rather than private ends may be recharacterized as a requirement that state intervention operate to increase society's level of well-being rather than simply redistribute wealth or utility from one group or individual to another.

> *Question:* Suppose that, in *Midkiff,* the Court had *not* found that the concentration of Hawaiian lands in the hands of a few large landowners created monopoly power distorting land and rental prices. Instead, the Hawaiian legislature simply felt that large landholdings were inequitable and should be broken up and redistributed to a broader segment of the public. Would such a motivation be a "public purpose" justifying the exercise of the state's police power?

2. *Midkiff* indicates that a government taking must bear a "rational" relationship to the legislature's intended public purpose. The Due Process Clause similarly requires that state action be rationally related to a legitimate public objective. See *Lee Optical,* above. The Supreme Court also has read the Equal Protection Clause to require state classifications to be rationally related to a public purpose. See United States Department of Agriculture v. Moreno, 413 U.S. 528, 93 S.Ct. 2821, 37 L.Ed.2d 782 (1973) (striking down federal law restricting foodstamp eligibility to households of related individuals on the ground that the restriction bore no rational

connection to the foodstamp statute's public purposes, but only to the impermissible purpose of discriminating against "hippies").

Professor Cass Sunstein has argued that "[t]he rationality requirement may * * * be understood precisely as a requirement that regulatory measures be something other than a response to political pressure" by rent-seeking interest groups. Sunstein, Interest Groups in American Public Law, 38 Stan.L.Rev. 29, 49 (1985).

Question: How much protection does the rationality requirement provide against welfare-reducing redistributive state action?

6. TAKINGS AND THE REQUIREMENT OF COMPENSATION

LORETTO v. TELEPROMPTER MANHATTAN CATV CORP.

Supreme Court of the United States, 1982.
458 U.S. 419, 102 S.Ct. 3164, 73 L.Ed.2d 868.

MARSHALL, JUSTICE.

This case presents the question whether a minor but permanent physical occupation of an owner's property authorized by government constitutes a "taking" of property for which just compensation is due under the Fifth and Fourteenth Amendments of the Constitution. New York law provides that a landlord must permit a cable television company to install its cable facilities upon his property. N.Y. Exec.Law § 828. In this case, the cable installation occupied portions of appellant's roof and the side of her building. The New York Court of Appeals ruled that this appropriation does not amount to a taking. Because we conclude that such a physical occupation of property is a taking, we reverse.

* * *

On appeal, the Court of Appeals * * * ruled that the law serves a legitimate police power purpose—eliminating landlord fees and conditions that inhibit the development of CATV, which has important educational and community benefits. Rejecting the argument that a physical occupation authorized by government is necessarily a taking, the court stated that the regulation does not have an excessive economic impact upon appellant when measured against her aggregate property rights, and that it does not interfere with any reasonable investment-backed expectations. Accordingly, the court held that § 828 does not work a taking of appellant's property. * * *

* * *

In *Penn Central Transportation Co. v. New York City,* the Court surveyed some of the general principles governing the Takings Clause. The Court noted that no "set formula" existed to determine, in all cases, whether compensation is constitutionally due for a government restriction of property. Ordinarily, the Court must engage in "essentially ad hoc, factual inquiries." But the inquiry is not standardless.

The economic impact of the regulation, especially the degree of interference with investment-backed expectations, is of particular significance. "So, too, is the character of the governmental action. A 'taking' may more readily be found when the interference with property can be characterized as a physical invasion by government, than when interference arises from some public program adjusting the benefits and burdens of economic life to promote the common good."

As *Penn Central* affirms, the Court has often upheld substantial regulation of an owner's use of his own property where deemed necessary to promote the public interest. At the same time, we have long considered a physical intrusion by government to be a property restriction of an unusually serious character for purposes of the Takings Clause. Our cases further establish that when the physical intrusion reaches the extreme form of a permanent physical occupation, a taking has occurred. In such a case, "the character of the government action" not only is an important factor in resolving whether the action works a taking but also is determinative.

* * *

Teleprompter's cable installation on appellant's building constitutes a taking under the traditional test. The installation involved a direct physical attachment of plates, boxes, wires, bolts, and screws to the building, completely occupying space above and upon the roof and along the building's exterior wall.

* * *

Our holding today is very narrow. We affirm the traditional rule that a permanent physical occupation of property is a taking. In such a case the property owner entertains a historically rooted expectation of compensation * * *. We do not, however, question the equally substantial authority upholding a State's broad power to impose appropriate restrictions upon an owner's *use* of his property.

* * *

The judgment of the New York Court of Appeals is reversed, and the case is remanded for further proceedings not inconsistent with this opinion.

It is so ordered.

BLACKMUN, JUSTICE, dissenting.

* * *

Before examining the Court's new takings rule, it is worth reviewing what was "taken" in this case. At issue are about 36 feet of cable one-half inch in diameter and two 4" X 4" X 4" metal boxes. Jointly, the cable and boxes occupy only about one-eighth of a cubic foot of space on the roof of appellant's Manhattan apartment building. * * *

* * *

The Court's recent Takings Clause decisions teach that *nonphysical* government intrusions on private property, such as zoning ordinances and other land-use restrictions, have become the rule rather than the exception. Modern government regulation exudes intangible "externalities" that may diminish the value of private property far more than minor physical touching. Nevertheless, as the Court recognizes, it has "often upheld substantial regulation of an owner's use of his own property where deemed necessary to promote the public interest."

* * *

* * * [Section] 828 differs little from the numerous other New York statutory provisions that require landlords to install physical facilities "permanently occupying" common spaces in or on their buildings. As the Court acknowledges, the States traditionally—and constitutionally—have exercised their police power "to require landlords to * * * provide utility connections, mailboxes, smoke detectors, fire extinguishers, and the like in the common area of a building." * * *

* * * For example, New York landlords are required by law to provide and pay for mailboxes that occupy more than five times the volume that Teleprompter's cable occupies on appellant's building. If the State constitutionally can insist that appellant make this sacrifice so that her tenants may receive mail, it is hard to understand why the State may not require her to surrender less space, *filled at another's expense,* so that those same tenants can receive television signals.

For constitutional purposes, the relevant question cannot be solely *whether* the State has interfered in some minimal way with an owner's use of space on her building. Any intelligible takings inquiry must also ask whether the *extent* of the State's interference is so severe as to constitute a compensable taking in light of the owner's alternative uses for the property. * * *

* * *

I would affirm the judgment and uphold the reasoning of the New York Court of Appeals.

Notes and Questions

1. *Loretto* held that when the state physically and permanently occupied a citizens' property, a taking had occurred and the state must pay just compensation under the Fifth and Fourteenth Amendments. Outside the context of a permanent physical occupation, however, the question of what amounts to a taking demanding compensation is muddled. As Justice Blackmun noted in his dissent, virtually every state regulation interferes with private property to some degree. Regulatory restrictions on the use one can make of one's property can impose a far greater degree of hardship than the minimal physical occupation in *Loretto.* At the same time, "[g]overnment could hardly go on if to some extent values incident to property could not be diminished without paying for every such change in the general law." Pennsylvania Coal Co. v. Mahon, 260 U.S. 393, 413, 43 S.Ct. 158, 159, 67 L.Ed. 322 (1922).

In Penn Central Transportation Co. v. New York City, 438 U.S. 104, 98 S.Ct. 2646, 57 L.Ed.2d 631 (1978), the Supreme Court reviewed a New York statute designed to preserve architectural landmarks by restricting the owner's ability to remove or alter landmark features without the approval of the New York Landmarks Preservation Commission. Penn Central, the owner of Grand Central Terminal in New York City, arranged a long-term lease with a developer which planned to build a 55-story tower atop the Terminal. Penn Central was to receive $3 million a year under the lease. However, the Landmark Preservation Commission refused to grant permission for such an alteration and Penn Central sued, claiming that the Commission's decision deprived it of property without compensation.

Justice Brennan's opinion for the majority noted that the question of whether or not such regulation amounted to a taking was an "essentially ad hoc, factual" inquiry. Among the relevant factors to be considered were "[t]he economic impact of the regulation, especially the degree of interference with investment-backed expectations" and "the character" of the governmental action: a physical invasion was more likely to be found a taking than regulatory interference with an owner's use. Ultimately, the Court held that Penn Central's loss did not amount to a taking requiring compensation.

Question: Penn Central suggests that the state can adopt regulations that impose severe economic losses on groups or individuals without paying for those losses. From an efficiency perspective, what risks are presented by such a rule?

2. In Nollan v. California Coastal Commission, 483 U.S. 825, 107 S.Ct. 3141, 97 L.Ed.2d 677 (1987), property owners sought to overturn a decision by the Coastal Commission that conditioned the granting of a permit to rebuild their beach home upon their providing the public with a right-of-way across their beach. The owners claimed that the state's action was not mere regulation but instead amounted to a taking requiring compensation. Justice Scalia, writing for the majority, held that the permit system amounted to a taking. He also indicated that when reviewing state regulation of land uses, the Court ought to apply a standard of review higher than the mere rationality required by the Due Process and Equal Protection Clauses. In particular, the Court ought to examine whether the regulation "substantially advances" (rather than being merely "rationally related to") legitimate state interests. See 483 U.S. at 835 n.3, 107 S.Ct. at 3147 n.3.

3. When the state does take property in a fashion that requires compensation, that compensation must be "full." In a dissent in *Penn Central,* Justice Rehnquist stated that "[t]he Fifth Amendment does not allow simply an approximate compensation but requires 'a full and perfect equivalent for the property taken.'" 438 U.S. at 150, 98 S.Ct. at 2672.

Question: Why is it important that compensation for a government taking of private property be a "perfect equivalent"?

4. Recall the Supreme Court's declaration in Hawaiian Housing Authority v. Midkiff, above, that even with full compensation, takings may only be made for a public use.

Question: Assuming as Justice O'Connor did in *Midkiff* that "the weighty demand of just compensation has been met," does requiring a public justification for a government taking improve the efficiency of state action?

5. The U.S. Constitution was drafted by prosperous, propertied individuals with full knowledge of their relative place in society.

Question: If the Takings Clause does not serve efficiency goals, is there another reason why the Framers might have included that provision in their Constitution?

7. STRICT SCRUTINY AND FUNDAMENTAL RIGHTS

SHAPIRO v. THOMPSON

Supreme Court of the United States, 1969.
394 U.S. 618, 89 S.Ct. 1322, 22 L.Ed.2d 600.

BRENNAN, JUSTICE.

These three appeals were restored to the calendar for reargument. Each is an appeal from a decision of a three-judge District Court holding unconstitutional a State or District of Columbia statutory provision which denies welfare assistance to residents of the State or District who have not resided within their jurisdictions for at least one year immediately preceding their applications for such assistance. We affirm the judgments of the District Courts in the three cases.

* * *

There is no dispute that the effect of the waiting-period requirement in each case is to create two classes of needy resident families indistinguishable from each other except that one is composed of residents who have resided a year or more, and the second of residents who have resided less than a year, in the jurisdiction. On the basis of this sole difference the first class is granted and the second class is denied welfare aid upon which may depend the ability of the families to obtain the very means to subsist—food, shelter, and other necessities of life. * * * [A]ppellees' central contention is that the statutory prohibition of benefits to residents of less than a year creates a classification which constitutes an invidious discrimination denying them equal protection of the laws. We agree. The interests which appellants assert are promoted by the classification either may not constitutionally be promoted by government or are not compelling governmental interests.

Primarily, appellants justify the waiting-period requirement as a protective device to preserve the fiscal integrity of state public assistance programs. It is asserted that people who require welfare assistance during their first year of residence in a State are likely to become continuing burdens on state welfare programs. Therefore, the argument runs, if such people can be deterred from entering the jurisdiction by denying them welfare benefits during the first year, state programs to assist long-time residents will not be impaired by a substantial influx of indigent newcomers.

* * *

We do not doubt that the one-year waiting-period device is well suited to discourage the influx of poor families in need of assistance. An indigent who desires to migrate, resettle, find a new job, and start a new life will doubtless hesitate if he knows that he must risk making the move without the possibility of falling back on state welfare assistance during his first year of residence, when his need may be most acute. But the purpose of inhibiting migration by needy persons into the State is constitutionally impermissible.

This Court long ago recognized that the nature of our Federal Union and our constitutional concepts of personal liberty unite to require that all citizens be free to travel throughout the length and breadth of our land uninhibited by statutes, rules, or regulations which unreasonably burden or restrict this movement. * * *

We have no occasion to ascribe the source of this right to travel interstate to a particular constitutional provision. It suffices that, as Mr. Justice Stewart said for the Court in *United States v. Guest:*

> "The constitutional right to travel from one State to another ... occupies a position fundamental to the concept of our Federal Union. It is a right that has been firmly established and repeatedly recognized.
>
> "... (The) right finds no explicit mention in the Constitution. The reason, it has been suggested, is that a right so elementary was conceived from the beginning to be a necessary concomitant of the stronger Union the Constitution created. In any event, freedom to travel throughout the United States has long been recognized as a basic right under the Constitution."

Thus, the purpose of deterring the in-migration of indigents cannot serve as justification for the classification created by the one-year waiting period, since that purpose is constitutionally impermissible. * * *

* * *

* * * [A] State may no more try to fence out those indigents who seek higher welfare benefits than it may try to fence out indigents generally. Implicit in any such distinction is the notion that indigents who enter a State with the hope of securing higher welfare benefits are somehow less deserving than indigents who do not take this consideration into account. But we do not perceive why a mother who is seeking to make a new life for herself and her children should be regarded as less deserving because she considers, among others factors, the level of a State's public assistance. Surely such a mother is no less deserving than a mother who moves into a particular State in order to take advantage of its better educational facilities.

* * *

Appellants next advance as justification certain administrative and related governmental objectives allegedly served by the waiting-period requirement. They argue that the requirement (1) facilitates the planning of the welfare budget; (2) provides an objective test of residency; (3) minimizes the opportunity for recipients fraudulently to receive payments from more than one jurisdiction; and (4) encourages early entry of new residents into the labor force.

At the outset, we reject appellants' argument that a mere showing of a rational relationship between the waiting period and these four admittedly permissible state objectives will suffice to justify the classification. * * * [I]n moving from State to State or to the District of Columbia appellees were exercising a constitutional right, and any classification which serves to penalize the exercise of that right, unless shown to be necessary to promote a *compelling* governmental interest, is unconstitutional.

* * *

Under this standard, the waiting-period requirement clearly violates the Equal Protection Clause.

* * *

Accordingly, the judgments in [these three appeals] are

Affirmed.

Notes and Questions

1. Following the demise of *Lochner* substantive due process, the Supreme Court has generally upheld legislative action under the Due Process Clause if it was rationally related to a legitimate public objective. The Court usually has applied a similar rational relation standard to government classifications under the Equal Protection Clause. See *Lee Optical* Question 7 and *Midkiff* Questions 1 and 2, above.

However, under both the Due Process and Equal Protection Clauses, state action or classifications that burden the exercise of a "fundamental right" have been held to the higher standard of strict scrutiny. The Equal Protection Clause also has required strict scrutiny when the state employed a "suspect classification." The strict scrutiny standard requires that legislation and classifications be "necessary" to a "compelling" government objective. Strict scrutiny appears to require both a greater degree of public interest to justify state intervention *and* a tighter causal link between that interest and the legislature's chosen means of pursuing it.

Justice Brennan's opinion for the majority in *Shapiro* struck down the welfare statutes at issue under strict scrutiny because their minimum residency requirements burdened a fundamental "right to travel" implied in the Constitution. What rights are or are not "fundamental" is not always obvious. The Court regularly has held that rights explicitly guaranteed by the Constitution, such as the First Amendment freedoms of assembly and of speech, are fundamental and legislation burdening those rights is subject to strict scrutiny under the Due Process and Equal Protection Clauses. However, the Court also has held that the Constitution implies other fundamental rights not expressly provided for in that document. See *Shapiro,* above (right to travel); Skinner v. Oklahoma, 316 U.S. 535, 62 S.Ct. 1110, 86 L.Ed 1655 (1942) (fundamental right to marriage and procreation); Griswold v. Connecticut, 381 U.S. 479, 85 S.Ct. 1678, 14 L.Ed.2d 510 (1965) (right to privacy in use of contraceptives); Cruzan v. Director, Missouri Department of Health, 497 U.S. 261, 110 S.Ct. 2841, 111 L.Ed.2d 224 (1990) (implied right to die rather than continue in persistent vegetative state). Still other rights have been held "fundamental" in the sense that, while the state had no obligation to provide that right, having elected to do so it could not discriminate among classes in a manner inconsistent with the Equal Protection Clause. See Harper v. Virginia Board of Elections and Kramer v. Union Free School District, above (discriminatory voter qualifications).

The Warren Court inclined toward broadening the concept of fundamental rights. The modern Court has been reluctant to expand the concept of fundamental rights beyond the cases that form the Warren Court's legacy. See *U.N. Declaration of Human Rights* Question 1, above.

2. Consider whether there might be economic justifications for according fundamental rights greater protection against legislative incursion than other rights. Rawls has argued that individuals negotiating a social contract behind a veil of ignorance will allocate political liberties equally, and will not tolerate differences in the level of political liberty society's members enjoy. See *U.N. Declaration of Human Rights* Question 1, above. Arrow's Theorem suggests that a legislature acting under majority rule may pass laws that impose greater disutility on the dissenting minority than the utility those laws provide to the approving majority. See *Kramer* Questions 3 and 5, *Bowers* Question 4, above. Judge Posner has argued that "[t]he nonpolitical rights in the Constitution (some of them are in it, though, only by judicial interpretation) are more plausibly regarded as a particularly durable form of legislative protection obtained by particularly effective interest groups * * *." R. Posner, Economic Analysis of Law 585 (3d ed. 1986). As an example, Posner suggested that the First Amendment may be viewed as "a form of protective legislation on behalf of an interest group consisting of intellectuals, publishers, journalists, pamphleteers, and others who derive pecuniary and nonpecuniary income from publication and advocacy." *Id.*

Question: How do each of the above approaches explain strict judicial scrutiny for statutes burdening fundamental rights while statutes burdening other rights need only meet the rational relation standard?

3. *Shapiro* held that a fundamental right to travel freely from one state to another was implicit in the U.S. Constitution. Justice Brennan argued that the right to interstate travel applied without regard to a citizen's motive for moving: a mother who moves to obtain a higher level of public assistance is "no less deserving than a mother who moves into a particular State in order to take advantage of its better educational facilities."

Question: How might a fundamental right to travel promote overall social welfare? Consider the differing implications of a right freely to exit any state and a right freely to enter any state.

8. STRICT SCRUTINY AND SUSPECT CLASSIFICATION

REGENTS OF UNIVERSITY OF CALIFORNIA v. BAKKE

Supreme Court of the United States, 1978.
438 U.S. 265, 98 S.Ct. 2733, 57 L.Ed.2d 750.

POWELL, JUSTICE.

This case presents a challenge to the special admissions program of the petitioner, the Medical School of the University of California at Davis, which is designed to assure the admission of a specified number of students from certain minority groups. * * *

* * *

Allan Bakke is a white male who applied to the Davis Medical School in both 1973 and 1974. In both years Bakke's application was considered under the general admissions program, and he received an interview. [In both years Bakke's applications were rejected.] * * *

* * * In both years, [black, Mexican–American, and Asian] applicants were admitted under the special program with grade point averages, MCAT scores, and benchmark scores significantly lower than Bakke's.

After the second rejection, Bakke filed the instant suit in the Superior Court of California. He sought mandatory, injunctive, and declaratory relief compelling his admission to the Medical School. He alleged that the Medical School's special admissions program operated to exclude him from the school on the basis of his race, in violation of his rights under the Equal Protection Clause of the Fourteenth Amendment * * *.

* * *

* * * Because the special admissions program involved a racial classification, the [California] Supreme Court held itself bound to apply strict scrutiny. * * * [T]he California Court held that the Equal Protection Clause of the Fourteenth Amendment required that "no applicant may be rejected because of his race, in favor of another who is less qualified, as measured by standards applied without regard to race." * * *

* * *

The guarantees of the Fourteenth Amendment extend to all persons. Its language is explicit: "No State shall ... deny to any person within its jurisdiction the equal protection of the laws." * * * The guarantee of equal protection cannot mean one thing when applied to one individual and something else when applied to a person of another color. If both are not accorded the same protection, then it is not equal.

Nevertheless, petitioner argues that the court below erred in applying strict scrutiny to the special admissions program because white males, such as respondent, are not a "discrete and insular minority" requiring extraordinary protection from the majoritarian political process. *Carolene Products Co.,* 304 U.S., at 152–153 n. 4. This rationale, however, has never been invoked in our decisions as a prerequisite to subjecting racial or ethnic distinctions to strict scrutiny. Nor has this Court held that discreteness and insularity constitute necessary preconditions to a holding that a particular classification is invidious. These characteristics may be relevant in deciding whether or not to add new types of classifications to the list of "suspect" categories or whether a particular classification survives close examination. Racial and ethnic classifications, however, are subject to stringent examination without regard to these additional characteristics. * * * Racial and ethnic distinctions of any sort are inherently suspect and thus call for the most exacting judicial examination.

This perception of racial and ethnic distinctions is rooted in our Nation's constitutional and demographic history. The Court's initial view of the Fourteenth Amendment was that its "one pervading purpose" was "the freedom of the slave race, the security and firm establishment of that freedom, and the protection of the newly-made freeman and citizen from the oppressions of those who had formerly exercised dominion over him."

* * * [It is] no longer possible to peg the guarantees of the Fourteenth Amendment to the struggle for equality of one racial minority. * * * [T]he United States [has] become a Nation of minorities. Each had to struggle—and to some extent struggles still—to overcome the prejudices not of a monolithic majority, but of a "majority" composed of various minority groups of whom it was said—perhaps unfairly in many cases—that a shared characteristic was a willingness to disadvantage other groups. As the Nation filled with the stock of many lands, the reach of the Clause was gradually extended to all ethnic groups seeking protection from official discrimination. * * *

* * *

* * * Because the landmark decisions in this area arose in response to the continued exclusion of Negroes from the mainstream of American society, they could be characterized as involving discrimination by the "majority" white race against the Negro minority. But they need not be read as depending upon that characterization for their results. It suffices to say that "[o]ver the years, this Court has consistently repudiated '[d]istinctions between citizens solely because of their ancestry' as being 'odious to a free people whose institutions are founded upon the doctrine of equality.' "

* * *

We have held that in "order to justify the use of a suspect classification, a State must show that its purpose or interest is both constitutionally permissible and substantial, and that its use of the classification is 'necessary . . . to the accomplishment' of its purpose or the safeguarding of its interest." The special admissions program purports to serve the purposes of: (i) "reducing the historic deficit of traditionally disfavored minorities in medical schools and in the medical profession," (ii) countering the effects of societal discrimination; (iii) increasing the number of physicians who will practice in communities currently underserved; and (iv) obtaining the educational benefits that flow from an ethnically diverse student body. It is necessary to decide which, if any, of these purposes is substantial enough to support the use of a suspect classification.

If petitioner's purpose is to assure within its student body some specified percentage of a particular group merely because of its race or ethnic origin, such a preferential purpose must be rejected not as insubstantial but as facially invalid. Preferring members of any one group for no reason other than race or ethnic origin is discrimination for its own sake. This the Constitution forbids. * * *

The State certainly has a legitimate and substantial interest in ameliorating, or eliminating where feasible, the disabling effects of identified discrimination. * * *

We have never approved a classification that aids persons perceived as members of relatively victimized groups at the expense of other innocent individuals in the absence of judicial, legislative, or administrative findings of constitutional or statutory violations. * * * Without such findings of constitutional or statutory violations, it cannot be said that the government has any greater interest in helping one individual than in refraining from harming another. Thus, the government has no compelling justification for inflicting such harm.

* * *

Petitioner identifies, as another purpose of its program, improving the delivery of health-care services to communities currently underserved. It may be assumed that in some situations a State's interest in facilitating the health care of its citizens is sufficiently compelling to support the use of a suspect classification. But there is virtually no evidence in the record indicating that petitioner's special admissions program is either needed or geared to promote that goal. * * *

* * *

* * * As the interest of diversity is compelling in the context of a university's admissions program, the question remains whether the program's racial classification is necessary to promote this interest.

* * *

The experience of other university admissions programs, which take race into account in achieving the educational diversity valued by the First Amendment, demonstrates that the assignment of a fixed number of places to a minority group is not a necessary means toward that end. * * *

* * *

It has been suggested that an admissions program which considers race only as one factor is simply a subtle and more sophisticated—but no less effective—means of according racial preference than the Davis program. A facial intent to discriminate, however, is evident in petitioner's preference program and not denied in this case. No such facial infirmity exists in an admissions program where race or ethnic background is simply one element—to be weighed fairly against other elements—in the selection process. * * *

In summary, it is evident that the Davis special admissions program involves the use of an explicit racial classification never before countenanced by this Court. It tells applicants who are not Negro, Asian, or Chicano that they are totally excluded from a specific percentage of the seats in an entering class. No matter how strong their qualifications, quantitative and extracurricular, including their own potential for contribution to educational diversity, they are never afforded the chance to compete with applicants from the preferred groups for the special admissions seats. At the same time, the preferred applicants have the opportunity to compete for every seat in the class.

The fatal flaw in petitioner's preferential program is its disregard of individual rights as guaranteed by the Fourteenth Amendment. Such rights are not absolute. But when a State's distribution of benefits or imposition of burdens hinges on ancestry or the color of a person's skin, that individual is entitled to a demonstration that the challenged classification is necessary to promote a substantial state interest. Petitioner has failed to carry this burden. For this reason, that portion of the California court's judgment holding the petitioner's special admissions program invalid under the Fourteenth Amendment must be affirmed.

* * *

Brennan, Justice, concurring in the judgment in part and dissenting in part.

* * *

* * * Since we conclude that the affirmative admissions program at the Davis Medical School is constitutional, we would reverse the judgment below in all respects. Mr. Justice Powell agrees that some uses of race in university admissions are permissible and, therefore, he joins with us to make five votes reversing the judgment below insofar as it prohibits the University from establishing race-conscious programs in the future.

* * *

Unquestionably we have held that a government practice or statute which restricts "fundamental rights" or which contains "suspect classifications" is to be subjected to "strict scrutiny" and can be justified only if it furthers a compelling government purpose and, even then, only if no less restrictive alternative is available. But no fundamental right is involved here. Nor do whites as a class have any of the "traditional indicia of suspectness: the class is not saddled with such disabilities, or subjected to such a history of purposeful unequal treatment, or relegated to such a position of political powerlessness as to command extraordinary protection from the majoritarian political process."

* * *

On the other hand, the fact that this case does not fit neatly into our prior analytic framework for race cases does not mean that it should be analyzed by applying the very loose rational-basis standard of review that is the very least that is always applied in equal protection cases. * * * Instead, a number of considerations—developed in gender-discrimination cases but which carry even more force when applied to racial classifications—lead us to conclude that racial classifications designed to further remedial purposes " 'must serve important governmental objectives and must be substantially related to achievement of those objectives.' "

* * *

[R]ace, like gender and illegitimacy, is an immutable characteristic which its possessors are powerless to escape or set aside. While a classification is not *per se* invalid because it divides classes on the basis of an immutable characteristic, it is nevertheless true that such divisions are contrary to our deep belief that "legal burdens should bear some relationship to individual responsibility or wrongdoing," and that advancement sanctioned, sponsored, or approved by the State should ideally be based on individual merit or achievement, or at the least on factors within the control of an individual.

* * * [I]t is clear from our cases that there are limits beyond which majorities may not go when they classify on the basis of immutable characteristics. Thus, even if the concern for individualism is weighed by the political process, that weighing cannot waive the personal rights of individuals under the Fourteenth Amendment.

In sum, because of the significant risk that racial classifications established for ostensibly benign purposes can be misused, causing effects not unlike those created by invidious classifications, it is inappropriate to inquire only whether there is any conceivable basis that might sustain such a classification. Instead, to justify such a classification an important and articulated purpose for its use must be shown. In addition, any statute must be stricken that stigmatizes any group or that singles out those least well represented in the political process to bear the brunt of a benign program. * * *

Davis' articulated purpose of remedying the effects of past societal discrimination is, under our cases, sufficiently important to justify the use of race-conscious admissions programs where there is a sound basis for concluding that minority underrepresentation is substantial and chronic, and that the handicap of past discrimination is impeding access of minorities to the Medical School.

* * *

Accordingly, we would reverse the judgment of the Supreme Court of California holding the Medical School's special admissions program unconstitutional and directing respondent's admission, as well as that portion of the judgment enjoining the Medical School from according any consideration to race in the admissions process.

MARSHALL, JUSTICE.

* * *

Three hundred and fifty years ago, the Negro was dragged to this country in chains to be sold into slavery. Uprooted from his homeland and thrust into bondage for forced labor, the slave was deprived of all legal rights. It was unlawful to teach him to read; he could be sold away from his family and friends at the whim of his master; and killing or maiming him was not a crime. The system of slavery brutalized and dehumanized both master and slave.

* * *

While I applaud the judgment of the Court that a university may consider race in its admissions process, it is more than a little ironic that, after several hundred years of class-based discrimination against Negroes, the Court is unwilling to hold that a class-based remedy for that discrimination is permissible. In declining to so hold, today's judgment ignores the fact that for several hundred years Negroes have been discriminated against, not as individuals, but rather solely because of the color of their skins. It is unnecessary in 20th-century America to have individual Negroes demonstrate that they have been victims of racial discrimination; the racism of our society has been so pervasive that none, regardless of wealth or position, has managed to escape its impact. The experience of Negroes in America has been different in kind, not just in degree, from that of other ethnic groups. It is not merely the history of slavery alone but also that a whole people were marked as inferior by the law. And that mark has endured. The dream of America as the great melting pot has not been realized for the Negro; because of his skin color he never even made it into the pot.

These differences in the experience of the Negro make it difficult for me to accept that Negroes cannot be afforded greater protection under the Fourteenth Amendment where it is necessary to remedy the effects of past discrimination. * * *

* * *

It is because of a legacy of unequal treatment that we now must permit the institutions of this society to give consideration to race in making decisions about who will hold the positions of influence, affluence, and prestige in America. For far too long, the doors to those positions have been shut to Negroes. If we are ever to become a fully integrated society, one in which the color of a person's skin will not determine the opportunities available to him or her, we must be willing to take steps to open those doors. I do not believe that anyone can truly look into America's past and still find that a remedy for the effects of that past is impermissible.

* * *

BLACKMUN, JUSTICE.

* * *

It is worth noting, perhaps, that governmental preference has not been a stranger to our legal life. We see it in veterans' preferences. We see it in the aid-to-the-handicapped programs. We see it in the progressive income tax. We see it in the Indian programs. We may excuse some of these on the ground that they have specific constitutional protection or, as with Indians, that those benefitted are wards of the Government. Nevertheless, these preferences exist and may not be ignored. And in the admissions field, as I have indicated, educational institutions have always used geography, athletic ability, anticipated financial largess, alumni pressure, and other factors of that kind.

I add these only as additional components on the edges of the central question as to which I join my Brothers Brennan, White, and Marshall in our more general approach. It is gratifying to know that the Court at least finds it constitutional for an academic institution to take race and ethnic background into consideration as one factor, among many, in the administration of its admissions program. * * *

* * *

Notes and Questions

1. Justice Powell announced the judgment in *Bakke* affirming the California Supreme Court's ruling that the Davis special admissions program was unlawful and that Bakke should be admitted to the medical school. However, Powell also reversed the California court's order enjoining Davis from ever giving any consideration whatsoever to race in its admission process. Only Justice Powell thought that the California Supreme Court should be reversed in part and affirmed in part. Justices Burger, Stewart, Rehnquist and Stevens concurred in the first part of the judgment but would have upheld the California Court's finding that race should never be a factor in medical school admissions. Justices White, Brennan, Marshall and Blackmun agreed with Powell that under some circumstances race might constitutionally be considered in admissions, but thought that Davis' particular special admissions program should be upheld. As a result Justice Powell had a majority (five votes, including his own) on each issue.

Question: How does the *Bakke* decision reflect the median voter theorem? See *Tashjian* Question 3, above.

2. Under the Equal Protection Clause, judges have applied strict scrutiny not only to state acts that burden "fundamental rights" but also to programs employing "suspect classifications." Racial classifications are

the paradigm of "suspectness." See Loving v. Virginia, 388 U.S. 1, 87 S.Ct. 1817, 18 L.Ed.2d 1010 (1967). The Court has also suggested that classifications based on national origin are suspect, Hernandez v. Texas, 347 U.S. 475, 74 S.Ct. 667, 98 L.Ed. 866 (1954), as are some classifications based on alienage, Graham v. Richardson, 403 U.S. 365, 91 S.Ct. 1848, 29 L.Ed.2d 534 (1971). In addition, the Court has identified certain classifications as "quasi-suspect." See Craig v. Boren, 429 U.S. 190, 97 S.Ct. 451, 50 L.Ed.2d 397 (1976) (gender), Levy v. Louisiana, 391 U.S. 68, 88 S.Ct. 1509, 20 L.Ed.2d 436 (1968) (illegitimacy). While quasi-suspect classifications have not been held to strict scrutiny, the Court has applied an intermediate level of review requiring the state's action to be "substantially" related to an "important" governmental objective. Craig v. Boren, above. Justices Brennan, Marshall, White and Blackmun thought the intermediate standard appropriate for classifications that worked to the disadvantage of whites.

As Justice Blackmun's concurrence noted, government preferences are common in American political life. When a classification is not suspect or quasi-suspect, it need only meet the rational relation standard. The Court has held that classifications based on age or wealth are not "suspect" and need not meet strict scrutiny. See Massachusetts Board of Retirement v. Murgia, 427 U.S. 307, 96 S.Ct. 2562, 49 L.Ed.2d. 520 (1976) (age); San Antonio Ind. School District v. Rodriguez, 411 U.S. 1, 93 S.Ct. 1278, 36 L.Ed.2d 16 (1973) (wealth).

> *Question:* Is there any reason to believe that preferences based on suspect classifications like race are more likely to be redistributive than wealth maximizing? Consider Justice Powell's assertion that the United States is a nation of "various minority groups of whom it was said * * * that a shared characteristic was a willingness to disadvantage other groups."

3. *Bakke* discusses a number of competing rationales for when a classification should be regarded as suspect. The petitioner in *Bakke* argued that the Court should test "suspectness" according to the famous footnote four of United States v. Carolene Products Co., 304 U.S. 144, 152 n.4, 58 S.Ct. 778, 783 n.4, 82 L.Ed. 1234 (1938). Justice Stone observed in that note that "prejudice against discrete and insular minorities may be a special condition, which tends seriously to curtail the operation of those political processes ordinarily to be relied upon to protect minorities, and which may call for correspondingly more searching judicial inquiry."

> *Question:* Recall the analysis of interest groups' roles in the political process in the questions following *Lee Optical,* above. Is Justice Stone correct in arguing that the fact that a minority is "discrete and insular * * * tends seriously to curtail the operation of those political processes ordinarily to be relied upon to protect minorities?"

4. Another factor the *Bakke* Court considered in deciding whether or not a classification was suspect was whether the classification was based on an "immutable" characteristic. See concurring opinion of Justices Brennan, Marshall, White, and Blackmun. Race, gender, and illegitimacy are immutable; wealth, veteran's status, residence, and smoking are not.

Question: From an economic perspective, is there any reason to suspect that classifications based on immutable characteristics are more likely to be welfare-reducing than classifications based on characteristics over which the individual has more control?

5. Justice Marshall's concurring opinion emphasized another factor in weighing suspectness—history. Marshall argued that because of the legacy of slavery, classifications that discriminate against blacks in favor of whites or other groups were more suspect than classifications that discriminate against whites in favor of blacks. Extrapolating from Marshall's historical analysis, the Court should uphold classification schemes that benefit Americans of African descent while it should strike down similar programs to benefit Americans of European, Hispanic, or Asian descent.

Question: Does Justice Marshall's analysis lead to welfare-enhancing rules?

Index

References are to Pages

References are to Pages

†